THE SPEED TECHNIQUE
TO ALPHA MEDITATION
AND VISUALISATION

The Speed Technique to Alpha Meditation and Visualisation

HAROLD KAMPF

With a Foreword by
Colin Wilson

quantum

LONDON NEW YORK TORONTO SYDNEY

quantum

An imprint of W. Foulsham & Co. Ltd.,
The Publishing ~House, Bennetts Close,
Cippenham, Berkshire, SL1 5AP

ISBN 0-572-02155-0

Designed and typeset in Great Britain by Peter Constable Consultants Limited.

Printed in Great Britain by St Edmundsbury Press Ltd., Bury St Edmunds, Suffolk.

Contents

*The greatest discovery in our generation
is that human beings,
by changing the inner attitudes of their minds,
can change the outer aspects of their lives.*

WILLIAM JAMES

Foreword

Harold Kampf is a personnel manager by trade, a writer by inclination – he has published ten books, mostly novels. In 1975, he sent me a small book called IN SEARCH OF SERENITY – A GUIDE TO SUCCESSFUL MEDITATION. My initial reaction was rather negative – I am not fond of 'How to Do It' books on meditation, yoga, self-hypnosis and so on. But as soon as I causally opened the book, I knew this one was different. He was obviously a man who knew exactly what he was talking about. I happened to open it at a paragraph labelled 'Seeing Angels', and this intrigued me. Mr Kampf had apparently become interested in the techniques of Subud, that interesting system of meditation brought to England by Pak Subuh in 1957. The essence of Subud is a method called the *latihan,* an 'opening up' of the mind that permits divine energies to operate. Harold Kampf was admitted to the *latihan* by a man who had been initiated by Subuh himself. Subuh seems to have been able to transmit some kind of current of vital energy – as Gurdjieff also had. John Bennett, the Gurdjieff follower who introduced Subud to England, declared that he saw angels during the *latihan*. Kampf comments:

'No, really, I thought! This is a strain on credibility. And one evening during Latihan *I too saw angels. I hardly dare to set it down – yet I know it was so, even though my two angels were quite unlike angels I might have imagined. They were like Grecian temple maidens, clothed in shimmering blue. In the* latihan *I was not overawed, but calmly accepted their appearance as quite a natural and understandable thing.'*

A man who could admit to seeing angels without embarrassment was obviously a down-to-earth sort of person, not the kind of irritating phoney who so often sets himself up in California as a teacher of meditation. So I turned to the beginning of the book, and found that Mr Kampf was indeed the kind of person I could trust – a man who had read a lot about meditation as well as practising it, and who knew what all the authorities had to say.

Another thing that interested me was that he attached basic importance to the idea of God without being, apparently, in any sense 'religious'. For Kampf, God was the creative energy of the universe, the Life Force. This again was refreshing. As a teenager I had been drawn under the spell of Shaw, and regarded him as one of the greatest men of the twentieth century. But all British 'intellectuals' seem to take it for granted that Shaw is hardly worth the trouble of dismissing. It still seems to me self-evidently true that the basic drive behind the force we call life is the desire to create deeper consciousness, a mirror in which it can become aware of itself. In Harold Kampf's world-view I immediately sensed something strongly akin to my own.

In fact, I came upon my own name on page 28 of his book. After citing a semi-mystical experience of the nature writer Richard Jefferies, he mentions that these sensations were what the psychologist Abraham Maslow (about whom I wrote a book) called 'Peak Experiences'.

The passage of Jefferies he mentions is more than a mere description of a 'peak experience' – which Maslow defined as simply an experience of bubbling, overflowing happiness. Jefferies says:

'Sometimes I have concentrated myself, and driven away by continued will all sense of outward appearances, looking straight with the full power of my mind inwards on myself. I find "I" am there; an "I" I do not wholly understand or know . . . Recognising it, I feel on the margin of a life unknown . . . on the verge of powers which if I could grasp could give me an immense breadth of existence, an ability to execute what I now only conceive.'

We may recall that the Scottish philosopher David Hume stated that when he looked inside himself for the 'real David Hume' he merely glimpsed a lot of ideas and impressions. For the next two centuries, Hume's denial of the 'essential self' became a cornerstone of western philosophy; everybody took it for granted – at least until the advent of a remarkable German thinker, Edmund Husserl, who pointed out that when I look *at* something, I *fire* my attention at it as an archer fires and arrow. If you let your attention drift as you read this page, you will simply fail to take it in – and that is as if the archer was too tired or lazy to pull back the bowstring, and the arrow fell in front of him to the ground. And a bow and arrow implies an archer, an 'I' who fires the arrow. Apparently Richard Jefferies had the ability to look deep inside himself and catch a glimpse of the archer who hides behind the facade of consciousness – the being Kant called the Transcendental Ego.

This is an important insight. It means that if David Hume failed to see the archer when he looked inside himself, it was because he was not making the same effort that Jefferies made. In Robert Anton Wilson's book ILLUMINATUS, someone remarks to a sage that when he looks inside himself he cannot see his essential 'self'; the sage replies:

'Who is doing the looking?'

Here we begin to move into the realm of Buddhistic insight, the sudden moment of enlightenment when we grasp the fact that we are not mere passive creatures of circumstance, leaves blown on the wind. We have real power to act, to do. And this is again a central recognition of an important philosopher: the German Fichte, a contemporary of Kant. Fichte noticed that when you sit in an armchair, merely thinking, you often feel a total nonentity. (Everyone has had that experience of reading for much too long – or watching television – and beginning to experience a sense of utter collapse, a feeling of suffocation.) But the moment I launch myself into determined *action,* this sense of boredom and suffocation vanishes; I feel a real person once more.

This is the feeling that all good teachers induce in their pupils – and it applies particularly to teachers of ideas. And it is something I felt as soon as I began to read the typescript of this new book by Harold Kampf.

Kampf soon makes us aware that in order to know certain basic secrets about living your life you do not need to be some kind of an 'adept'. The secret itself is what matters, and it really works.

I found myself reading the book with increasing excitement. It brought back to me my own 'initiation' into such matters, at the age of seventeen. I was a typical adolescent intellectual, reading everything I

13

could lay my hands on, yet always feeling bored, inadequate and clumsy. Like T. E. Lawrence, I envied a soldier with his girl, or a man patting his dog, because they seemed to belong to the real world, to nature, not to some intellectual twilight zone. Then, through a reference in one of T. S. Eliot's essays, I came across the *Bhagavadgita*, the Hindu scripture that teaches how a man should learn to know himself. The hero, Arjuna, is about to lead his army into battle against an army in which there are many of his friends and relatives; he bursts into tears and says he cannot do it. Then his teacher, Krishna, tells him that his mind is worried and confused by illusions. He must exercise total detachment, and cease to care about the results of his actions. The only way to avoid suffering is to rise above the confusion of desires and anxieties that seem to constitute the warp and waft of human life. He must recognise that his essential being is immortal, made of the same substance as God.

I began to practise meditation, as taught in the *Gita*. I learned to regard the adolescent 'me', trapped in his sense of awkwardness and incompetence, as a kind of illusion. Recognising that a part of my sense of will-lessness was due to inactivity, I began getting up early in the morning, and jogging for an hour, then walking to work instead of taking the bus. The result was that I had a sudden sense of control over myself and my own life. I felt I was changing myself, turning myself into a different person. Whenever I had a chance, I would find a quiet place and sit cross-legged, my attention concentrated, my gaze 'fixed at the root of the eyebrows'. And it was like 'pulling myself together'; after ten minutes, I felt refreshed and full of energy.

There are, I later discovered, many different methods and systems of achieving some degree of self-control. I found that the Christian mysticism of Eckhart and Suso led in precisely the same direction as the serene meditation of Buddhism or Taoism – or, for that matter, the shock tactics of Zen. I realised that Socrates was aiming at the same kind of detachment through the use of the powers of reason, and that Marcus Aurelius achieved it through Stoic disciplines. And when I came upon Gurdjieff – in Ouspensky's IN SEARCH OF THE MIRACULOUS, I realised that he attempted to combine many forms of discipline in his notion of self-observation and 'the war against sleep'. It made no difference which way one chose. The really important moment was the recognition that we can choose to alter ourselves, that even though all our habits of thought try to conceal it from us, we are masters of our own lives.

The way of Nietzsche's ZARATHUSTRA may seem very different from the way of St John of the Cross, but they are based upon the same optimistic insight: that we are stronger than we think. We do not have to be slaves of the trivial; the mind can be turned, like a searchlight, onto more important things.

Wells's Mr Polly said:

'If you don't like your life, you can change it.'

And the corollary is: If you don't like yourself, you can change that too.

Then why bother to read THE SPEED TECHNIQUE TO ALPHA MEDITATION AND VISUALISATION when the 'way' to inner freedom has been known for thousands of years? Because our age has seen immense advances in the knowledge of the actual *mechanisms* of the mind. For example, the realisation that we have two people living inside our heads, one in the left and one in the right half of the brain – and that the left-brain is the 'you' – can provide the basis for a new insight into the problems.

It would be absurd to say:

'I don't want to know about such things because Socrates or Buddha did very well without them . . .'

What Harold Kampf has accomplished here is an exciting – and totally personal – synthesis of techniques that seem to range from traditional yoga to the 'visualising' disciplines of the Cabbalah and the relaxation techniques of transcendental meditation. No one – no matter how much he knows about such things – can fail to gain new insights from it.

The down-to-earth Mr Kampf has brought a refreshing new approach to one of mankind's oldest problems; that, in itself, is a life's achievement.

Colin Wilson

Why Do It?

CABBAGE OR COLESLAW?

Basically coleslaw is cabbage with mayonnaise added, plus a few simple refinements to make it even better and tastier. But it is still cabbage at heart.

Do you want to remain cabbage or become coleslaw?

Most people have wanted to change something about themselves at some stage of their lives. They don't want to change basically, just lose or change bad habits or improve one's image (become more likeable, attractive, confident), improve one's ability to perform (as a worker, an artist, a musician, a writer), play sport better, be healthier . . .

Anyone can achieve any of these things and the simplest, easiest way is by visualisation, but (and this is where most methods come to grief) this is only truly effective if done in *Alpha*. There are many books that will tell you to visualise things, or to sit and breathe in this or that way, and, it is hoped, you will achieve a meditative state one day with patience, or to concentrate your breath, to stare at a candle flame, to go from colour to colour, and so on. I have tried them all. Eventually, almost despairingly, I devised my own Whole-person Deep Level Technique and taught it with some success. The formula for this will appear later in the book. However, once I discovered the A-B-C method I realised that this was the ultimate method to achieve the Alpha state speedily and easily.

You can make assertions if you like, such as:

'I am calmer, nothing can affect my equilibrium; I am daily becoming less irritable; my heartbeat is calm and regular; my warts are disappearing; my golf swing is improving every day.'

But just imagine how many hundred times more effective those statements must be if at the same time you 'see' in your mind these improvements taking place. At the Alpha level! What the person can 'see' is what he or she becomes.

WHY ALPHA?

You probably know the recognised brain rhythms of Beta, Alpha, Theta and Delta. Their speeds are approximately:

Beta 14 to 28 cycles per second

Alpha 8 to 13 cycles per second

Theta 4 to 7 cycles per second

Delta 0.5 to 3 cycles per second

Beta is our normal waking state, while Alpha is the slower rhythm (but with greater awareness) which is normally attained in meditation, self-hypnosis (or auto-suggestion), and hypnosis – although it is, of course, possible to reach lower brain rhythms in each of these. Theta often mixes with Alpha and is the next deeper state, while Delta is the usual sleep state and mixes with Theta cycles. To work on oneself, the Alpha state is sufficient, at least certainly to start with.

DE-MYSTIFICATION OF MEDITATION

The main purpose of this book is to de-mystify the subject of meditation and self-hypnosis – or auto-suggestion – as well as setting out how to achieve this state in the fastest possible way.

Why fast? Because many people are put off these 'disciplines' by the long exercises considered necessary to reach them. Some teachers feel it is important to take time to learn the techniques, in order to prove one's seriousness, if nothing else. They contend that it is only when you are prepared to spend time that you deserve the prize of self-help.

I believe otherwise. I believe that the more people there are who practise meditation the better the world will become. Here I must mention that this applies both to passive meditation and to dynamic meditation, which is the one for changing or working on oneself. These will be detailed in the next chapters.

A STEPPING-STONE

The Sufis claim that everything in life is a stepping-stone to its inner purpose – whose chief aspects are the desire to live, to have knowledge, to attain power, happiness and peace. This seems to be a reference to power over one's self and not to the usual power over others.

Despite the multitudes of people it is in some ways rather a lonely world into which we are born. At times we wonder why we are here and whether life is a joke, an accident or perhaps merely a creative experiment. We ask ourselves whether existence has any purpose, any real meaning. To most people life appears to be a struggle. The normal security of our childhood fades away. Certainly we live and work together for mutual benefit and comfort, but because of the way we've structured the world we're all in competition with one another. We aim at being the biggest or the best, the most beautiful, the richest, the most influential or powerful; or we pretend not to care

21

if we fall by the wayside. Whichever the case, we wear masks to hide our real selves, masks because we feel too vulnerable without them.

Harvey Stack Sullivan, the famous psychologist, called masks our 'security operations', designed to protect an already damaged ego from further vulnerability. For instance, a sensitive person, afraid of being hurt, may wear a sardonic, callous mask. Yet behind our masks we feel a certain emptiness, a need for reassurance, for we are all full of fears and uncertainties.

A wise man once said:

'He is truly liberated who is free from desire, fear and anger.'

A very difficult state to achieve.

BASIC EMOTIONS

Perhaps our most basic emotion is fear. Everything else seems to spring from it. Love, for instance, only comes after fear has been conquered. As for desire (wanting what we haven't got and fearful we won't get), that's fairly basic too. Desiring starts right down from our lowest needs of food and shelter, and, moving up the scale, to wanting esteem from others. We decide that in order to acquire these things we have to act in certain ways. When we find these work we wear the masks that show us the kind of person we want others to think we are. Unfortunately others don't always read our masks properly, or else we don't always paint them on very successfully.

As to resentment and anger, when people won't accept our masks, or don't like them, resentment is born. Anger is much the same. Terribly destructive emotions!

'I get angry very quickly,' says someone with pride, and one shudders for the speaker. What wonderful lives we could all have if we were free from those three monsters – fear, desire, anger.

Pride is an offshoot from desire and fear. If we weren't afraid of being thought inferior, unworthy, we wouldn't trouble to wear a pride mask.

MAIN AIMS IN LIFE

Someone has said that our main aims in life are to avoid pain and to experience pleasure. Pain, whether mental or physical, is to be feared and avoided while pleasure is to be actively sought. But what is pleasure? Is it love, security, comfort, status? Many people think of it as a single objective, for example a visit to the theatre or cinema, the act of getting married, falling in love or into bed, a football match, a party. Yet in fact every single objective of pleasure, once it has been reached, no longer satisfies. There is only one permanent satisfier: a feeling of serene joy or real contentment. But is that a true possibility?

It is for many people, if they want it enough. We are not, of course, all at the same stage of development but a tremendous number of people are ready for that, to live in peace and happiness, if they could only learn to improve the quality of their lives. There are, of course, those who argue that if we had no conflict and competition life would be boring and there'd be no progress. This is a specious argument for we are born with a creative urge, and being happy frees and enhances our ability to be creative. One might enquire whether our Creator requires conflict to be creative.

What then, one may ask, of evil. Is there not always the conflict of good versus evil? How does this concept fall into place in our quest?

Those who have heard or read Paul Solomon may remember that when his 'guides' were asked to define 'God' they said it was *the Power that could envisage good without reference to evil*.

Do you follow the concept? No 'Good versus Evil'. When I use passive meditation I say to myself, *There is only God; there is only God's Power,* by which I mean I do not believe that any evil force can exist unless man himself accepts it as a separate force, and so, for himself, grants it power. I believe this 'mantram' that I say protects me from the concept of evil.

In our fear-ridden society, how then does one go about casting out fear? How do we stop being afraid?

A quotation says: *'Perfect love casteth out fear.'*

Christ commands us to love one another and gives us the golden rule *'Do unto others as you would have them do unto you'*. (From this I devised my own 'karmic' rule: *'Whatever you do unto others will be done unto you.'*) Confucius had a similar 'Rule of Reciprocity' - called *Shu* in Chinese: *'Do not do unto others what you do not want others to do unto you.'*

These commands seem difficult but not so impossible for those who know we are all part of one great consciousness.

WHAT IS LOVE?

If we accept that loving gets rid of fear, we have to begin asking what love is. My dictionary defines it as an intense emotion of affection, warmth, fondness and regard towards a person or thing. To aim at this one would have to emulate Mother Teresa, a difficult task indeed; she might even tend an ailing Hitler with concern, whereas most of us would consign him for ever to outer darkness. But we could at least start by trying to find the good qualities in our fellow beings and try to excuse the ignorance that makes them seem unlovable. Few are Hitlers and few have no redeeming traits whatsoever. Often sympathising and understanding open the door to loving. One can love that which is lovable and this gives space for what is not lovable to change in them. It is not so difficult then to start sending out affection, warmth and regard to others.

If one was always loving one would be at peace; one could not then be greedy, desiring what someone else had. One would be so secure in oneself that there could be nothing to fear.

THE PROCESS OF CHANGE

To start this process is simple enough: one needs to *change*

Simple? Or not? Happiness, remember, is freedom from fear, desire and anger. And all three of these emotions come in some way from others, from what other people do or say. Although our problem may seem to be other people, it is in fact our *reaction* to other people. It is wanting something from others – be it approval, security, sex, or whatever. That's what gives others the power to hurt us, for us to hurt ourselves. Yet our only true security is from within. Just think about wanting something badly and not getting it – whether it's approval, or promotion, or even love; that's what hurts us. Yet whatever it is, you don't really *need* it, it is not *essential* for your survival, for your happiness. It is your false self that has been wanting these things, the self that has been competitive and demanding. That same self neglects to tell you that if and when you do get what you've been demanding and wanting you still won't be happy. Oh, for a short while you'll be pleased, excited. Then you have to find a new peak. Excitement is not happiness.

Yes, if you chase happiness, when you've caught it – why, it's gone again. To be truly happy is to be content in every moment.

'To catch the winged joy as it flies . . .' as William Blake put it. To be happy is to be yourself always. Not to have hunger for approval, for acceptance. That is real freedom.

HAPPINESS

Happiness is *inner* freedom from fear, and anger and anxiety. It has nothing to do with anyone else; no one can either give it to you or withdraw it from you. When you give up your dependency on others you become independent and confident. When you are at peace within yourself you are freed from what others think or do: you alone are in charge. You have enough without the riches or glamour of others.

But some believe that we are bound to strive for more. Did not Christ, they ask, rebuke the man who made little use of his talents?

Strive for more *what?* Not money, not goods, not girls! Not material things! Only immaterial things such as knowledge, wisdom, love, and an improvement of your talents. Yes, indeed, every one of us has some special talents, something unique to offer. What we have to do is recognise them and foster and develop them – do the absolute best we can with them. It doesn't have to be a big talent – we're not all going to be concert pianists. It doesn't even mean that sort of talent necessarily. You might have a talent for communicating well with children, of being a good housewife, of being a good messenger – or even lavatory cleaner for that matter. We should never envy those who seem rich or strong; they only seem so, but in some other way or another they too are weak and suffering. Health, perhaps – or trouble at home. They all wear masks too. But when a 'real' person appears, he or she makes those who wear masks seem ridiculous by contrast; it is easy to see that such a person has no need to wear a mask.

Now, as to change, there comes a time when we just have to sit down quietly and be a little analytical about ourselves and, most of all, honest. We shall talk more later on about self-analysis and essential goals. However, if we're seriously considering some sort of change in ourselves then we must first face ourselves honestly, truthfully. We must take a good calm look and examine our inner goals: not to be a king, but to be at peace; not to be 'successful', whatever that may mean, since success is only in the eye of the beholder (when anyone reaches success, it has already moved further on), not to be that but to be harmonious, i.e. to be in harmony with the universe, to do what you want but also to want what you do, to do your best work and to be a loving person.

OUR INNER GOALS

We can now summarise our goals:

- To get rid of your old self.
- To heal yourself (we are not talking about physical health just now).
- To be your true self, healthy in mind and ways, independent but having good relationships with others.

Such a programme brings peace and happiness, an abiding contentment. Could one ask for more?

Possibly not – but one may ask whether contentment supplies a reason for living? Not really, though it is likely that one will come to a reason when one's mind is at peace because then one becomes aware of a force beyond ourselves. It is true that you can live peacefully even when you believe life to be an accident. But when you realise that life leans towards good rather than evil, when you examine yourself and see your need to develop harmoniously, why then you probably are here to do just that, to grow.

INNER GROWTH

Growth is learning. A first step might be to recognise when we do wrong – to be aware when we are doing something 'ugly', as a child I know put it so beautifully. But to do something ugly and just not care: that's hardly a forward step. So we grow mainly in our attitudes towards others, in consideration, in compassion, in unselfishness.

It is difficult to be unselfish and caring when you are unhappy. But, of course, we are unhappy when we are at odds: desiring, fearful, anxious, resentful, angry. So, again, if we are not afraid of whatever anyone says or does, then we no longer desire, become fearful, anxious, resentful or angry.

Can we really remake ourselves, in effect create our own lives afresh? Yes, we can, almost like an artist creating a picture from scratch. People often blame their parents, their inherited genes and their environment for their faults, and, of course, these conditions may have been formative factors. However, there comes a time when you have to say:

'I'm on my own. What's past is past but I'm starting afresh right now, and from now on it's up to me.'

After that, why, you have a wonderful blank

piece of paper to draw yourself on. Easy to say, but it does mean giving up the bad habits and traits of a lifetime.

A CASE HISTORY

Before explaining the mechanics of changing, it might be useful to look at a case history. This is the story of Kathy.

Kathy was troubled about her marriage and the way she put it was that she felt she was losing her identity. She was a pretty girl and did not have to worry much about her looks. Not that looks are as important as some girls think; it's what lies behind the looks that is important. Any girl or woman can present attractiveness when she puts out her femininity, not as a weapon but as part of her true, natural, loving self.

Kathy was married to Harry, a man who, she thought later, was not particularly interested in her. Now when things go wrong in a relationship, when there's disagreement, many women want to talk it through, analyse and digest it, and give the situation a good workout. Often men, however, don't like this. What has happened is, to them, just a disagreement – perhaps there has even been a flare-up, but then it is all over. It's finished now and things are fine again. But unfortunately the female partner may see that as a lack of interest.

This may sound a simple – even petty – thing, but in fact it can become very serious. Kathy was sensitive not only to her husband but to her friends and relatives too. Her father was a big drinker; they'd always been close even though Kathy didn't like his appetite for alcohol or his behaviour when he became drunk.

Recently he had embarrassed her husband when Harry had taken him to a special function. Harry had been furious both with her father and herself – because he was her father – but the next day he was over it. Kathy, however, had spent a sleepless night, angry with her father and feeling guilty towards Harry because it was after all her father who had caused the trouble, just when Harry was trying to be especially nice to him. She couldn't wait to talk it all out with her husband.

Then what did he do? He looked surprised, touched her gently on the shoulder in sympathy. But it was finished; he didn't want to discuss it, have a post-mortem. He was even more surprised when she then burst into tears. Obviously, she decided, if he didn't want to discuss something of such importance in their marriage, something which had caused him such rage, then their relationship couldn't mean much to him. It always happened like this, she said.

That was Kathy. She was swept along by the

actions and words and reactions of Harry and everybody else. When people couldn't understand how she felt about things, then she felt hurt and misunderstood and unsure of herself. She was very often in this unhappy state.

Now she set about changing things. First she analysed herself, decided on her assets and her liabilities. Her main assets were her looks. (But this was just a freak of nature and didn't help her anyway, she reasoned. In fact sometimes it was a disadvantage; people often thought that confidence went with good looks, whereas she often felt lonely inside and jelly-like.) Next, she had a kindness and general feeling of good will towards people, until she was 'rebuffed'. She had quite a good brain and a nice husband – only she wasn't sure he really cared about her.

Liabilities? Lack of confidence; too great a dependence, first on her father and then on her husband. This led to anger and resentment when they did anything to upset her, and a constant uneasy fear that something would transpire to break the calm. Because of her fear she was nervy and short with Harry and continually on the defensive. This attitude put him on the defensive and made him keep a distance between them, and he took to using sarcasm as a weapon.

They ran a business together but even here they

were becoming adversaries, competitors.

WHAT WAS THE SOLUTION?

First to calm herself physically and mentally. She learnt how to do this – we shall discover the method later on. She also realised she had to learn to be her true self, as nice looking as she could, at peace with herself, unselfish, able to use her mind constructively and creatively (as indeed she could when it was uncluttered with damaging emotions), thoughtful, considerate and caring. Those were her real values and in time became her face value too.

Kathy's problem was the one we all face. It was the question of: 'Who am I?' All her life she had allowed herself to be dependent on other people. She had wanted their understanding, their approval. This actually put her in their power. They had not asked for this but she gave them this right because subconsciously she thought that was her need. She now discovered it wasn't and she consciously withdrew that right. In effect she said: *'From now on I'm going to conform to my own standards and you must accept me as I am. If you reject me, that's okay with me.'*

She became strong enough to be able to say that. She realised that when you detach yourself from others they lose their power over you, that when you are complete, happy, joyful, loving, no one can disturb you, that if they do it is only because you give them the power to affect you.

It is rather like driving a car. Whatever idiotic thing (short of hitting you) that another driver does, it can only affect you if you give your permission. If you react, who does it affect? You. Your anger will hurt you but certainly not the other driver. If you think calmly: *'Poor fellow! I really feel sorry that he has to act like that; I'll try to send him some good vibrations and maybe he'll feel better,'* then you are in charge of the situation. It wasn't easy at first for Kathy to withdraw herself. But she learnt to 'watch' a painful emotion reaching her – anger, distress, fear, hurt – and then continue to watch it and deliberately withdraw from it, and so it would lose its power over her. The more she could control her emotions, the more power she had. She learnt to listen to people properly and to try to understand what was really happening between them and herself. When she neither expected nor demanded any special form of behaviour, she could never be disappointed. When she did not impose her standards on others she became more self-contained, more understanding and less judgemental. She learnt not to respond to people in a personal way, an emotional way. She was at last able to be herself, unique (as we all are) and genuine.

Perhaps you can *feel* how Kathy came to a new set of beliefs and a whole new way of life, but you want to 'see' how it happened, how the process actually took place. This will be shown a little later in the story of Frank. For the moment, let us look at the different kinds of meditation, at relaxation, and at self-hypnosis.

How It Works

RELAXATION

To go into Alpha requires relaxation of both the body and the brain. You will notice that I say brain and not mind. Mind is in total charge; it is *you*. It is mind that gives direction to the brain and the brain then instructs the body. Your mind is your 'director'; if you believe in immortality, we might describe your mind as your immortal essence.

You may wonder why it is necessary to relax physically, and the answer is that unless you do you cannot get the brain to relax. Another reason (part of the same, really) is the need to do away with tension or stress. When your body and brain are tense you cannot be calm and slip into Alpha. This is why it is so difficult to go into Alpha when you are troubled or in pain. But if you have accustomed yourself to meditating regularly you will be able to relax and go into Alpha in times of stress and so alleviate the situation.

WHAT STRESS IS

Since stress is one of the things we are aiming to avoid, we should perhaps talk about it.

Stress or tension seem to be a part of modern living but they can affect you adversely by causing chemical changes in both body and brain. Unfortunately too much stress affects the body's immune system. It can for instance inhibit the defence production of cancer-fighting cells. It can cause digestive problems, give you headaches or backache and even create the right body climate for a cold.

It affects not only people with high-pressure work but also those who have a demanding job but little decision-making in what they do, such as telephone operators, bus drivers, cooks and assembly-line workers; their minds seem to resent them becoming, to some extent, automatons.

Stress can also be caused simply by many small daily irritations, or by hostility. Anger is, of course, one's own worst enemy, affecting the angry person much more adversely than the recipient.

You may become stressed even without your conscious knowledge, by polluted air, by too much constant noise, by all the hazards of overcrowding, by too fierce competition without let-up. Feelings of anxiety, of low self-esteem, phobias, inability to cope, poor concentration and memory, accident-proneness, depression – all these can result from too much stress or tension.

Daily relaxation of brain and body can counteract these, lead you to take charge of your own life, and improve both its quality and your health. It pays to meditate.

BODY RELAXATION

This is not enough on its own to defeat all those potentially nasty things stress can do to you, though it helps. The A-B-C Technique automatically relaxes both body and brain, but if it is simply physical relaxation you are interested in, here are some methods you can employ.

You can drop onto the floor like a leaf and just lie there prone on your back, legs slightly apart and arms loosely by your sides.

You can also visualise yourself as a floating piece of seaweed drifting in with the tide. That helps, and you may go off to sleep for a few minutes and wake up tensionless. Do this periodically and it should help to restore your vigour – but it won't, of course, bring you any of the deeper benefits obtained by meditation or self-hypnosis.

The method of physical relaxation I used to teach as part of the meditative process was an abbreviated form of 'progressive relaxation', quickly tensing and relaxing every muscle. Preferably sitting upright but comfortably in a chair you breathe deeply in and out a couple of times, to calm the body. Then you tense your muscles progressively, as follows:

To concentrate better, close your eyes. Now you put your toes together, pigeon-toed, heels a little apart, and push your toes down into the floor. That tightens and tenses your foot and leg muscles. Next, tighten your thighs, tighten your buttocks, tighten your abdomen, trying to press it against the small of your back; tighten your shoulders, your chest, your back. Raise your arms, fists clenched, elbows stiff. Squeeze your eyes tight shut and clench your teeth. Keeping your face all tight and screwed up, arch your neck, point your chin up. Then you hold that feeling of tension right through your body, at the same time holding your breath. You hold it all for about seven seconds.

Now you let all that tension *explode* out of you. Let it flow out – your arms back to your sides, your chin down. Concentrate for a few seconds on feeling all the tension flowing out. Check out the muscles of the toes, legs, thighs. If there is any tension still there, release it, just let it go. Relax the muscles of your abdomen and back, the muscles of shoulders and arms and fingers – let them all feel nice and heavy – and the muscles of your face, your jaw, your eyelids, even your scalp. You take a deep breath, hold it, let it slowly out, and say to yourself: *'Relax, relax.'* Say to yourself: *'Whenever I instruct myself to relax, this is how I will feel.'*

After a while, with daily practice, you would be able simply to say, *'Relax, relax'*, and your body would automatically do everything for you.

While the description of this process sounds a bit long-winded, the carrying-out of it would only take about 30 seconds.

We shall come back to this and the consequent method of going into meditation – as an alternative to A-B-C, which I have called the Ultimate Technique. Some people may prefer one method to the other.

MEDITATION: PASSIVE AND DYNAMIC

Originally to meditate meant 'to think on', i.e. think about some subject and turn it inside out, to contemplate it deeply. Gradually it acquired a religious connotation and quite the reverse of actually thinking about anything at all. In fact it means giving one's mind over to God.

When I say 'God' you can if you wish substitute whatever word for a Higher Power you fancy.

The difference between passive and active or dynamic meditation in a nutshell is that with the latter, instead of handing your mind over to the Power of God, as we have said, you are consciously using your mind, at a deep level, to instruct your body and brain

41

to work on yourself (and even perhaps on others, for good only).

PASSIVE MEDITATION

If you do not believe in a Higher Power, although you can certainly be taught to go into Alpha, the experience will be largely purposeless except to relax your body and brain, and what you achieve will not be true meditation. However, you will, willy-nilly, be contacting your deeper, subconscious self. In time you may well expand your awareness, improve your creativity, and find yourself generally more at peace. Because you will become calmer you are likelier to become more healthy and free from the results of stress.

A consulting physician states that a meditation technique can assist the immune system when damaged by stress; physical relaxation is comparatively easy but the 'psychological dimension' eludes many people, and meditation helps provide this missing dimension, since 'it provides very deep levels of rest in both a physical and psychological sense'.

Some who have been on drugs find they can kick the habit. You may even be led to believe in a Power outside yourself, if your mind has a subconscious need for that. But if not, have no fear that you will be inveigled into spirituality. God is a closed shop and membership is open only to those who seek it.

'*What is there capable of surviving the cataclysm of death?*' asks Kenneth Walker in MY KEY TO LIFE. '*Only in moments of meditation when the everyday self is momentarily in abeyance do I catch a glimpse of the greater self, which is entirely different from the small, separate self of everyday life.*'

NEED FOR MEDITATION

Do we need passive meditation? By this I mean, of course, a contact with a Higher Power – or even a higher self. I always consider myself extremely fortunate in having a 'conversion experience' many years ago when I was in great personal need. While I was in some despair an inner voice suddenly expressed itself by telling me not to worry, to 'let go' and all would be well in due time. This experience was blindingly clear and real to me and I instantly knew that, contrary to my previous belief, life was part of an immortality, that worldly death was merely a step on the way, and that I was undoubtedly in the hands of higher forces than mine.

Without this knowledge I cannot think that I would so happily have succumbed to such a world as we live in. But since then supporting evidence has accumulated so fast that it is there for anyone to acquire and know. And if you meditate regularly with an open mind, jagged pieces of light constantly hurl themselves at you and enlarge your understanding.

WHAT DO YOU DO?

As Brother Mandus (THIS WONDROUS WAY OF LIFE) said:

'There is nothing to do! The Father does all that needs to be done. I say silently: "Here is my life, Father, all I am, all I possess; I lay it down for Thee. This moment, this day, eternally, Thy will, not mine." The silence in the Father's presence grows deeper as I practise coming to Him . . . We should not ask God for anything in the silence; it is the time for God to do all that needs to be done. Our only task is to allow Him to do it. If we do this it is absolutely amazing how all things for our joy are added upon us, pressed down and running over – love, wisdom, happiness, achievement, and supply.'

Could one ask for more?

As St Augustine said:

'I went round the streets and squares and cities of the world seeking Thee and found Thee not, because I sought without for Him who was within.'

Possibly the Christian churches have forgotten how important meditation is. A clergyman who read a previous book of mine (IN SEARCH OF SERENITY) on this subject said:

'It is such a pity we in the Church don't read and do more about this; we need to find the time.'

There is time enough for prayer, but true meditation is also a deep form of prayer.

What is it to pray?
It is to become one with God or with the Eternal.
To pray is to talk,
And the higher you go
The more silent your speech.

A well-known American seer told of visiting a youngster who was in prison and of speaking to him about religion. Later when he visited the boy he found him kneeling and repeating the alphabet slowly from beginning to end.

Curious, he asked the boy why he did this.

'Sir,' was the reply, *'if that man Jesus is as wise as you say, he knows better than me what I want to tell him.'*

We can see and sense the truth of this. If and when we pray it is usually to tell God what we want Him to do for us. Isn't the best prayer perhaps: *'I leave it to You'*?

When we are in meditation we indeed speak within our inmost silence and release our field of energy, our consciousness, to the great Life Force. And, following the law of all nature, what we give out returns to us in full measure and overflowing. As we may know, this applies to both good and ill. Thus the opening of ourselves, and the flow of energy so released, engenders a return force which may at times make us feel that we are within a veritable power house.

The truest prayer then is the silent meditative communion with the Creative Force. You have taken yourself out of the way; you have made yourself ready to receive the Power. You have come in silence and submission and you rest in stillness for whatever may appear.

When you feel this for yourself you will come to understand how the meditation of a few can change the attitudes of the many. In deep silent prayer or meditation one finds that one goes beyond the need for purely personal gain and development. One finds contact with and joins the Universal Force, of which all life is a part; one becomes a unity with It and with mankind as a whole. One becomes a channel, a sort of conduit pipe through which the Force can travel to all those who in any way come within one's consciousness.

EASE IN LEARNING

Till now meditation has always been considered to be long and difficult to learn and thus often avoided. Yet now the technique can be learnt quickly and easily.

It is available to all who want it. And in every religion it seems that meditation is found to be the one common factor necessary for spiritual progress. One might even say that without it one comes to a spiritual barrier: 'Thus far and no further!' We are like the man in the anonymous story of 'Footprints', which goes as follows:

One night a man had a dream. He dreamt he was walking along a beach with the Lord. Across the sky flashed scenes from his life. For each scene he noticed two sets of footprints in the sand, one belonging to him and the other to the Lord.

When the last scene of his life flashed before him he looked back at the footprints. He noticed that many times along the path of his life there was after all only one set of footprints. He also noticed that this happened at the very lowest and saddest times of his life. This really bothered him and he questioned the Lord about it.

'Lord, you said that once I decided to follow You, You would walk with me all the way. But I have noticed that during the more troublesome times of my life there is only one set of footprints. I do not understand why when I needed You most You would leave me.'

The Lord replied:

'My son, my precious child, I love you and would never leave you. During your times of trial and suffering,

when you see only one set of footprints, it was then that I carried you.'

The Trouble with God

GOD AND MEDITATION

While we are talking about passive meditation we ought not to beat about the bush but meet the question of spirituality head-on. As I have already said, if you are not ready for this, then it is not a problem for you. There is no reason why you should not learn to go quickly into Alpha and be in a meditative state and I will show you how to 'get' there and how to still your thoughts. Yet while we are here we should discuss the concept of 'God' for those concerned.

If the name itself is a problem, let us list some possible alternatives:

> Universal Intelligence,
> Omnipotent Mind,
> Universal Spirit or Power,
> Infinite Intelligence.

There are many alternatives.

The real trouble with God is that so many people still see Him as an entity – a superhuman. When we visualise God as a force, the Force, the Life Force that created and holds the universe together, then that's a different story. Another way of looking at it might be to say that God is law – the law of love, the law of creation, birth and rebirth – but not an entity that can be contacted and asked for things, to refashion or renew relationships, to change circumstances. The power for Good (God) is always there, always available when anyone opens him or herself to It.

Perhaps the most remarkable thing is that we can alienate ourselves from It as much as we like, do as we wish, yet when we finally call out to the Power in our distress, open ourselves to It, It is always there waiting for us, offering Itself to our acceptance; that is the real Grace of God. Lawrence LeShan puts it well when he says:

'It seems to me that the challenge to science, to man, to the human experiment, is finally and irrevocably whether or not man can accept that he is a part of the energy of the universe and can only function harmoniously within it through his capacity to love infinitely.'

From THE AQUARIAN CONSPIRACY comes this note: *'The more we learn about the nature of reality, the more plainly we see the unnatural aspects of our environment – and our lives. Out of ignorance, out of*

*arrogance, we have been working against the grain . . . Not
realising that our species evolved in co-operation, we have
opted for competition in work, school, relationships.'*

And this is indeed our world –
competitiveness, winning at all costs, the achievement
of power and possessions. The opposite is co-
operation, harmony, service to our fellow beings, and
the attempt towards unconditional love. It is a hard
road to travel alone, perhaps impossible without the
recognition of a Power that's stronger than you. When
you do move along this road, you strangely begin to get
an almost automatic co-operation from others too. The
reason is that you have then begun to be another sort
of person.

A MEDITATIVE EXPERIENCE

One day in meditation I had the strange feeling
of wanting to 'dissolve' myself. Somehow the sides of
my body had seemed to start dissolving and, enjoying
the feeling, I mentally encouraged my whole body to
do the same until finally I was just 'not there'. I felt that
I had become in a very real way a part of the Universal
Life Force. And every time for a while that I meditated
after that I began to repeat this experience deliberately.
You could put it another way and say I placed my body
on one side and surrendered my consciousness to
becoming one with my Source, or the one and only

Consciousness that we all are, that all things are. During these periods I deliberately linked up my consciousness with It, and when you do this the power you feel is phenomenal – because you are not only part of It, you *are* It.

Eileen Caddy puts it this way:

'Listen – listen – and then you cannot fail to hear that still small voice within you which is My voice, and the most wondrous gift which I hold out to all mankind . . .'

The feeling I had was in the 'going out' of me and the still small voice within me and yet also outside of me because I too was then outside. To me it seemed that I had returned, for that period of time, to the Power that created me and that this was really the answer to life.

For thousands of years we have been drifting away from the Power, thus creating the only real sin there is, the sin of separation. We were made by the Power, as part of Itself, and this is what is meant by man being created in God's image. Man's job, his purpose, was to experience life in the world for the Power – as Its extension. Everything was provided for him: health, abundance of all he needed, physical resources – they're always here for everyone who asks for them.

There really is enough, ample, for everyone, not when you ask, petition, but when you demand it *by*

Law, which means living your life in accordance with "the Law" and not merely your own desires.

However, when you choose to remain and live in separation you find a quality of life is lacking. Of course, sooner or later everyone does want to return to his or her Source. When this finally happens it can for some be too late. Not I think for ever because my belief is that we all have another chance, another time, even in another life.

Yet if you do 'hand over', say:

'I want You to live my life through me; please help me to get myself out of the way and just use me as a channel' – why, then it happens.

Everything falls into place and your life becomes meaningful, and then you can just live from day to day because you have become a definite part of a plan – only it's not your plan. You have handed over, and your faith and trust are never misplaced. Do not take it on my word, but what can it cost you to experiment? If you do, then quite simply, whatever happens to you – and it may not be what you expected or even hoped for – will be right for you, the best thing possible for your growth and development (*which is really what you are here for*), and yes, even for your eventual enjoyment and satisfaction, for you will know you are a very real part of the divine plan. There really has to be one, don't you think? Could all this intricacy of life be just an accident? Whatever nonsense there is in life can only ever be attributable to man! That must be the ultimate argument for those who blame the 'Almighty' for the Holocaust or whatever. Certainly there are at times 'natural' accidents ('Acts of God' the insurers call them) and at times nature itself seems a little barbaric, but we can only try to understand ourselves and not the Infinite. And finally, when you come to believe that life is eternal your perspective on our present existence becomes quite different.

THE EFFECT OF HANDING OVER

You will no doubt remember the biblical instruction '*Take no thought for the morrow*'. When you do that it does not mean you have now to pack up your own goals. You still have these, only you may well find your goals have changed, are changing, because of the new you now emerging. But you will be directed, put on the right path and required to carry on. You might think that now you have asked this Power to run your life you need *do* nothing further yourself. But of course it is not so. Just because you have handed over the plan for your life, it does not mean the plan can be executed by anyone except you. What you have really been saying is:

'*Show me what You want me to do, guide me, and give me the means, the tools, to do it.*'

HAPPINESS, THE INNER SECRET

We are nearing this now. As you see, it is a state which has nothing to do with other people; it concerns only the you within, the inner you. Being your own self now takes on a new meaning because it works in accordance with Divine Power and not merely your own. Being yourself in this way creates a self that is completely *other* supportive, dependent not on peer wishes but on your new 'centred' self. Because you are now listening to the 'inner music' you no longer fear the tunes of other people. You allow them to behave as they wish and you are free to be inner-confident, to be independent while also caring and compassionate. You will no longer fear failure, sickness, loneliness. Paradoxically, just because you hand over, you actually have more power to deal with things, not less.

One might ask, if Law is impersonal and cannot be petitioned, how can It be ever called upon? The answer is that since It provides everything you can ever need, and once you have accepted this and 'hand over', and not a minute before, you will draw everything to yourself. And you can actually claim It in this sort of fashion:

'All power, all consciousness, is at the centre of my being always, and draws unto me everything necessary for my good.'

If you say this daily, mentally in your

55

meditation it helps clear a channel for its fulfilment. And you yourself may be used (and glad to be used) to send power and help to others.

One wonders: how does this Power, Infinite Mind or Intelligence, or whatever, work? We don't really know, of course, but we must believe there is some hierarchy of helpers – not too difficult to believe once we accept an afterlife of some nature.

Life is energy and the transfer of energy (whatever its nature) and when your mind is centred on the one Power, the only Power, that knows your good, then that Power creates, materialises, your desires – having indeed first created those very desires in your mind.

Thus 'handing over' is the ultimate decision in your life. And what is it you really face? It can be a bit of a risk, can't it? After all, the whole thing may possibly be a fraud! It is because of this that people who live on logic alone just cannot do it, cannot accept it, cannot even think or talk about it. Their right brain hemispheres of intuition and inner listening have atrophied. Yet even they have inner dreams, to which they close their minds and to the divinity that is within them. They live in sadness, in denial of their true selves.

Yes, it is a risk, a leap in the dark. But what tremendous rewards are on offer: love, acceptance, support, inner knowledge, no feverish struggle to achieve, only the calm of *doing*, daily achievement, growth. The achievement by itself is no longer vital: the doing is all, bringing satisfaction and contentment. Certainly you must work towards your goals; nevertheless you must not worry about the results, must set no demands but just work harmoniously with hope, with optimism, with expectancy. When you do this you become freed, a free person. When all is well now, then it will be always well. The present moment is always now, not the past, not the future.

And if the results do not always appear good? That must not be allowed to matter. If one has done one's careful best, that is all that really matters, and the appearance is not always the answer. Living in this way, worry falls behind and fear goes out of the window: all is proceeding as it should. You are under the control of Infinite Power, and away from the control of human power. You can actually declare: '*I give this situation no power over me*'. 'Handing over' does not diminish you in any way. You are not in competition with your Source; you are its agent, its servant. The trouble is that some people do not want to be a servant, even of God's. '*Toughies!*' as a friend of mine says. Delusions of grandeur have a limit, and this is it. After all, they came here for a purpose – to develop spiritually, to grow in awareness, to recognise and use 'the kingdom within'.

People who are cruel and uncaring, who are all for self, can only destroy themselves, waste their lives. We can pity them because they do not know what they are doing to themselves. They are still asleep, unaware. They may have acquired worldly importance, but importance can be unimportant. Only what you really are is important.

When you meet such people you know that their apparent injustice towards you cannot hurt you if you are spiritually whole. Outward circumstances may be affected; inwardly just contact your Higher Force and hand over. You will be guided, you will be given strength, patience, wisdom, your path will be made smooth and straight. You need no one else in the last resort. Your own Guru is inside you.

CONTACTING YOUR HIGHER FORCE

Whether we want to achieve passive or dynamic meditation, we shall use the same A-B-C Technique. In the next chapter we will explore the two kinds of meditation.

Mind, Meditation and Visualisation

THE MIND

In Chapter 2 we discussed the first part of any practical meditation: relaxation of the body. Now we must learn to relax the brain, or even by-pass it. When I say that, it is really the left brain we have to by-pass because it is filled with logic (due to our way of civilisation) and is apt to be suspicious when the right brain needs to take over, as it really does in meditation where we use our intuitive senses. Ideally the two hemispheres should work together, as they will with practice in meditation.

The two hemispheres are of the cortex of the brain. The left side, in charge of such things as logic, and mathematics and science, has a 'critical censor', that is, a built-in detector of non-logic. It is this censor that the right hemisphere, largely using intuition and creative imagination, must avoid. Contrary to scientific thought, in life one has many times to suspend judgement and accept with Shakespeare that there are *'more things in life than are dreamt of in your philosophy'*.

Mind, as we have seen, is the real controller of the self, the essential 'I', the permanent personality. And it is 'I', the mind, that controls the brain and tells it what to do. If 'I' *don't* tell it, the brain will do all sorts of silly things on its own. If 'I' direct it, the brain will respond accordingly, particularly when it is operating at the Alpha rhythm; it will allow the right hemisphere of the brain to take over from the left when necessary. And the brain in turn controls the body.

Thus the sequence ends up with the body doing whatever it is that 'I', the mind, wants. This is why so many of us do, and become, what we don't want and don't like. People have over time given us the wrong feedback and we have accepted it and built on it so our brain and body act accordingly. We literally make ourselves ill because we think we deserve it.

POWER OF NEGATIVE THINKING

Suppose someone asks you how you are. You may say: *'Lousy.'* Your brain takes that as a literal order, that you desire to continue feeling lousy. Brain tells body and the instruction becomes reinforced. You begin to feel worse and worse. But if you respond, *'I feel fine,'* then your brain-body organisation takes it as an order that you want to feel good and the better you say you feel the better you will feel.

But can you say you feel fine if in fact you really feel lousy? Yes, indeed you can. Dale Carnegie claims that feeling follows action and he never said a truer word. If every morning you wake and tell yourself, *'How wonderful – a new day! This is going to be a wonderful day,'* then it will be so. If you wake each morning dreading getting up, afraid of the day and what it will bring, then it will be a bad day for you. Truly, the power of programming yourself in Alpha is tremendous. Soon we shall see how this can be achieved.

MEDITATION, MAKING THE CHOICE (OR SELF-HYPNOSIS)

Whichever one you choose at any particular time, it is still meditation. And if you practise T M or the Relaxation Response or watch your breathing or stare at a candle, don't be misled; these are merely techniques for 'getting you there', into the meditative state. They are not meditation *per se*. My Whole-person Deep Level Technique and the A-B-C Technique are still only techniques to start you meditating. It really does not matter how you get there, and that is why I have always looked for the simplest and quickest method of achieving this. 'There' is 'Alpha', which as you know is a lower brain rhythm, and when you are at this lower level you will be more aware than ever before. Some of the authors of techniques regard them as mystiques. I believe otherwise.

Now you have a choice. You can either sit passively and still your thoughts – I'll show you how – or you can use your brain dynamically to programme or reprogramme yourself. You will do this with visualisation. A third choice could be self-hypnosis (or auto-suggestion) which really means self-instruction in Alpha, but without visualisation. If you know anything about hypnosis, you will be aware that a hypnotist can assist you to go into a lower brain rhythm level (Alpha or even Theta) and then instruct you (brain and/or body) to respond to certain positive commands. You can do the same yourself once you are in Alpha, but generally the added use of visualisation is best.

WHAT IS VISUALISATION?

Whatever one can imagine, one can achieve! So visualisation is in fact imagination! The reason you must do this in Alpha is because of the strong concentration of the brain at that level. If you can think of the brain as a circle of casually floating cells or energy units, imagine a thought moving through the brain and hitting a random number of those units. A hit-and-miss method! But in Alpha the units are concentrated together in an orderly way so that a thought would go through each one of them and so have a more vital and more lasting result. In Alpha you in fact narrow the focus of your attention, whereas in Beta (our normal state) one cannot get one's brain to listen properly because there are too many conflicting claims on one's attention.

Even in the 'waking' state after a meditative session, the energy units will remain charged and will continue to carry their dose of suggestion. Each session will reinforce previous ones and a build-up of constructive energy is the result. Being able to achieve through imagining does not mean that one could thus claim all knowledge. That would be a ridiculous assumption. For instance, a lawyer could hardly imagine himself as an electronics engineer and then expect to be one. But with this technique of visualisation in Alpha he might expect to learn more easily how to become one, if his bent was that way.

The technique works because the human animal is geared to goal-seeking. Our automatic creative mechanism operates in terms of goals. Thus if you give it a definite goal to achieve, you can depend upon your automatic guidance system to take you to that goal – much better and faster than you could ever manage by conscious thought. But the goal must be seen so clearly that it becomes real to your brain and nervous system. This is what is meant by consciously creating circumstances; it is not only possible but it is what we do all our lives. Mostly we have a bumbling, fuzzy aim at something or other but the deliberate Alpha aim is the one that works best.

No Difference Between Experience and Imagination

Perhaps the last paragraph sounds more difficult than it really is. The fact is that your automatic mechanism just cannot tell the difference between an actual experience and one which is vividly *imagined*. The only information available to it concerning any given situation is what you believe to be true about it. And that is the whole kernel of visualisation. It is why, if we constantly picture failure to ourselves so vividly that it becomes real to our nervous system, we will be 'rewarded' with negative failure-type responses and emotions – and just the opposite when we picture ourselves successful and confident.

Your self-image is therefore your key to success or failure, adequacy or inadequacy. And if the image is inadequate, you must correct it, in Alpha and in the dynamic meditation process.

CAN EVERYONE VISUALISE?

Some people say they cannot use imagination or visualisation. When we deal with the practical techniques and the use of dynamic visualisation in Chapter 6, you will see that you can do it better than you might think.

All Change

FRANK'S CASE

While many people would like to be able to change themselves, it is difficult for them to know how to go about it. Frank's story may be able to illustrate a method for them.

At the age of 35 Frank was a real mess. He was separated from his wife and a young son. He was an alcoholic and in some ways a sick man. He had at times physically attacked his wife, but the reason she had left him now was fear for her infant son when an alcoholic spell occurred. Afterwards he could never remember what he'd done; in this way he switched off responsibility for his actions.

Frank was actually a very good salesman – he sold electric appliances and claimed to be able to sell ice to an Eskimo. However, when I first saw him he was bleary-eyed and hadn't shaved for a few days. Fortunately he was off drink at that time – an interim period. I found him to be a seething mass of contrary emotions, completely muddled and even possibly heading one day towards insanity of some kind.

He had had a domineering father and a nagging, drunken mother. At times he felt so inadequate and timid that he refused to go to work. He would take to his bed in a fit of depression and just lie there staring at the wall or ceiling. It is known of course that depression usually denotes an inner anger.

When Frank looked at you his eyes seemed to be saying unsayable things; at times you could almost see the cogs moving confusedly at first, but then clicking firmly into place.

Change? What *could* he do to change?

First he could stop drinking – if it were possible. Frank thought it was possible. As so many alcoholics do, he said:

'I can stop whenever I want. I do sometimes.'

When it was suggested that he went into an alcoholics' hospital he snorted derisively.

'I don't need them. I'm not a true alcoholic; I don't fall into their pattern at all.'

After a pause he said quietly:

'But I do know I've got to do something about myself.'

We talked for a while, particularly about his relationship with his parents. He was intelligent enough to see he'd been blaming them for everything that had happened to him and to realise that this just wouldn't work any more. When he had lost his father he had taken to another crutch (his mother's) – alcohol.

Dependency, fear, need – all his cravings and weaknesses stemmed from these. He really had to start to rethink himself right through, to take every item that posed a query and decide whether it was right or wrong for a new Frank. To be able to list all one's bad points honestly and fearlessly is not easy, especially when one has a very small catalogue of good points to set against them. Yet each bad point has an opposite and can become its reverse, if we want to make it so.

If Kathy's problem had been 'Who am I?' then Frank's problem was not only 'Who am I?' but also 'Where am I?' In other words, he needed to enquire why he was here at all – whether the world had any sort of meaning for him.

Frank put himself into the 'Self-examination Centre' and drew up a list when he was analysing himself. Heading the list was this note:

'This is only really for me, so I can be as caustic or sanctimonious as I like. And if my outreach is too high it's the fault of my counsellor, but I'm glad he's made me do it. Here is my 'Balance Sheet':

ASSETS

Physical health – Good

Traits/emotions – Feel
confident at times,
perhaps a false
confidence

Generous at times

Love – Not really able to love
another fully

LIABILITIES

Mental Health – Poor
– Depression
– Periodical craving for alcohol
– Feel inferior more often than
   not; hide this under aggression
– Selfish
– Need praise, approval
– Despise weak people (am I
   afraid of looking into mirror?)
– Paternalistic really, and only
   kind when I can 'afford' to be
   so generous
– Boastful
– Sometimes greedy
– 'Hard' in business
– Want my own way
– Impatient
– Afraid as hell of almost
   everything, and afraid of
   showing it
– Get very angry when thwarted
   or challenged; overbearing
– Afraid to trust, to let go
– Enjoy sex at times (though not
   at all when drunk) but as a
   pleasure for myself; not very
   concerned about my partner

STRATEGY OR GOAL TO BE ADOPTED

I can accept that I tend towards alcoholism and I shall join AA. All the above negative traits must be turned to positive.

RELATIONSHIPS
With parents

Hated my old man but afraid of him and obeyed him. My mother nagged me to distraction. She was afraid of him too, hence her drinking. I wasn't all that kind to her. Both dead now. I realise there's no use regretting the past. The best I can do for anything I've done wrong is to do better in the future.

With those at work

We're strictly in competition. It's always been either them or me and I never let it be them – I've always put myself first. I shall try to visualise myself acting in different ways. We'll see if consideration for others pays off in satisfaction; I can take that risk.

Customers

I've always given good service, because I know it pays best. But it's not from personal feelings of goodwill or caring. If I'm doing a good job I could do an even better one with concern for the customer's real needs.

(Questions re. work: What have I really been doing there? What would I really *like* to do there? What do I want to become?)

With family

When I read through my Liabilities I can see what my wife has had to put up with. Do I want her back or would I rather start afresh? But would starting afresh help? She stuck with me in the bad days and we could have a good life if I can really change myself. And the boy – we must give him a good home; I think we owe him that. So yes, I do want her back, and on her terms.

GENERAL ACTION TO BE TAKEN

I've got a few decent instincts but I always smother them when I feel them emerging, on the basis of: 'I have to look after No. 1 first'. If I can acquire more self-confidence, not just on the surface but really deep inside, then I won't have to be afraid of what other people think or say or do. I don't have to be in competition all the time, just do the best I can. Then I wouldn't have to be afraid of not getting or having things or the approval of others. And if people challenge me it won't really matter because *I* will know what's true or not. Nor does it really matter what others think of me – that's *their* business. If I do my best for my family and myself, and for others, then I can't do more. I can see that now. And if I can get and keep that inner peace, then I won't have anything to get angry about.

I've got the technique now on how to work on myself and things are starting to change. I do *want* to change – not to become saintly (joke!) but to be in control, to be my real inner self.

THE SECRET OF CHANGE

To simplify this to the utmost: if you're unhappy, find out what is wrong – and change it. Too simple? Not really. Just go one step at a time into visualisation through Alpha. Work on one item at a time – say for a week at a time – and see the changes developing. Anyone can change if they want to work at it – say two quarter-hour sessions a day (it isn't very onerous).

You can't achieve it by will-power, only by using your imagination and belief. As they say: 'What the mind can conceive and you can believe – you can achieve.' But if will and imagination come into conflict, imagination wins every time. To illustrate: try *not* to think of two very large lions for five minutes . . .

SELF-ANALYSIS

Do you recall the case of Kathy in Chapter 1?

Her problem was 'Who Am I?' She needed constant approval and she had to learn how to control her emotions. Well, she made her self-analysis (her 'Self-examination Centre') and then she decided exactly how she did want to be, and what kind of person. Through visualisation in Alpha she learnt to watch herself in various circumstances, and then she would replay the scenes as she would like them to have taken place. In this way she conditioned herself to changing her attitudes, her feelings and her actions. She said it was like restructuring, remoulding herself. She literally made herself over, the same person but different.

A useful way to start self-analysis is to record for a few days your reactions to people and events. First, you would make a list of all the negative qualities you can think of, such as fearfulness, anger, jealousy, resentment, pride, irritability, self-pity, hatred, criticising, judging, etc.

Now when any unpleasant incident occurs, you must note which one of those negative qualities is your reaction to it and ask yourself why you react as you do. If you're being honest you'll soon get a true picture of yourself. Whatever the other person says or does, only you are responsible for your reactions and, whenever you wish, you can change this picture.

It is usually our strong ego that makes us act negatively, and when we realise this we can prepare

73

selves to react differently in the future. One example
uld be reacting with anger (or self-pity) against
another's anger. This may unfortunately become a
continuing, even daily, state of affairs. Now we can
observe the other's anger, and perhaps even discover
just why it occurs. But we can certainly learn not to
react to it with our own anger.

In Frank's case it was much the same, but
perhaps he had even more problems. His main one was
how to acquire more self-confidence (in place of drink)
and becoming the sort of person he'd really like to be.
He also needed to learn how to handle his anger. What
he did was not only to replay his scenes, as Kathy did,
but also play scenes actually in advance of their
happening. Mentally and visually he scheduled
contacts with people, including his wife, as he wanted
these to be, with him in control of himself. And his
scripts turned out much as he'd planned. He geared
himself and his behaviour for optimum response and
he got it. He also worked on getting his drinking under
control and in due course gave it up altogether.

REPROGRAMMING YOURSELF

Can an angry man – one who gets angry all the
time – can such a person stop being angry once he
discovers that it is literally poisoning his system (to say
nothing of his relationships)?

The point is that reason very seldom comes into the question of anger; it is emotion gone haywire, out of control.

The yogi adage says 'An ignorant man becomes angry; the wise man understands' – the wise man being one who understands himself first and, therefore, understands others.

When we snap back at others it is our touchy ego-self that makes us do it. But if we are calm inside we understand what is going on and so don't hit out. Now in order for the angry man to be able to achieve this state he must first reprogramme himself.

Let us assume that you have been through your own personal Self-examination Centre and will therefore know which items you want to re-programme. You will have started this process by looking at your self-image. In most people this has become set by the age of about six. Sounds a bit young, doesn't it? But it is so. If you have ever watched youngsters grow up you can see that basically they remain the same people they always were. Your good points do get reinforced but so do your bad ones (which is why no one should ever marry another with the thought that bad behaviour will miraculously improve; it will only worsen with familiarity). As to self-image, the truth is that everyone suffers from an inadequate one in some aspect or another.

The reason is that we all feel ineffective in certain areas and we believe we always will. In those areas we have fixated our bad points instead of trying to change them. As far as these are concerned we have literally programmed ourselves (usually with outside critical help) for negativity and failure.

When I look back at my own experience, I was patterned in shyness, a lack of self-confidence which had probably arisen from a severe hand and face injury – burnt under a mosquito net when I was tiny. When I had a job which at times demanded a certain amount of extroversion I forced myself to take a public-speaking course. I made myself mix freely with people, but it was a struggle.

Self-confidence, or the lack of it, is a good example for us because it applies to so many people. Often it is created by such a thing as parents unwittingly making a child feel small and inadequate.

'You're such a fool,' shouts father. Or: *'Why are you such a clumsy boy? Useless, aren't you?'*

Of course, there are many other ways it can come about, but in any event over the years the negativity gets reinforced by other incidents. Is it any wonder the chap becomes ineffective, or perhaps tries to make himself seem better by scoring off other people? I'm sure we all know many people who try to cover up their inadequacy in that way.

Frederick Bailes claims that timid or shy people are usually so because of unconscious hostility. Such a person may feel that others are against him, that for instance they will criticise him if he doesn't talk as well as they do. This keeps him silent. It also makes him a poor salesman. It makes him too introverted and apart from others. In a sense it is self-centredness because he is constantly thinking of himself, the impression he is making, the possible criticisms of others. He is afraid of being hurt. His love is going in and not outwards. What he needs is to shift his centre of attention towards others, ready to give of himself whatever the outcome.

Whatever the cause, that person knows of his inadequacy – his inadequate self-image – and now he must deliberately set out to change that self-image to the one of his choice. What he does is to 'see' the bad picture of himself – as he is, as he has been up to now. Then he cancels it, and follows it with the good picture of himself as he wants to be. And he continues to do this every day for at least a week until the new programming is 'set'. This is visualisation; it is not a new theory and several books teach it. When they fail they do so because they do not teach this: *It must be done in Alpha.*

When this is done, it works.

This is dynamic meditation in use. To sum up,

our aim is to deprogramme and then reprogramme ourselves. We have first accepted that everyone is the architect of his own future, that we are what we choose to be. By everything we do each day we create what is to come later. You have to forget the past. There is no use having guilty feelings, for what is done is done. If one can make amends – good. Do it and forget and forgive yourself. In other words, accept yourself as you are now and as you intend to become. Realise that past possibilities no longer exist, only future ones. You are going to create your new self-image as you desire to be.

You may have heard the saying *'To change what you get, you must change what you are!'* Remember that everything that exists physically has existed first in thought. Even such a mundane thing as a cake! So if we don't like the experience we have, we'll have to change the kind of thoughts we have. Changing our thought pattern will change our behaviour – and that in turn will change our future experiences.

We must therefore plan ourselves, our mental attitudes, and a whole improved personal world; we must create the right sort of goals and make a bee-line for them.

THE NEED FOR GOALS

If you don't have some goals in life, you are practically dead. People without any goals are simply asking for some disease to come and get them. It does not have to be a goal to change the world. But if one does not have some small goal, he had better set out to establish one. For example: 'to work for myself'; 'to do a part-time job'; 'to do some social work'; 'to be a good (or better) husband/wife'; or whatever.

And even in grief, over a loss, that is when one is vulnerable to any illness that the stress of the loss can aggravate. This is when one has to accept the inevitable, and not just fold one's arms. This is the time when one has to make a new goal. Even a small daily goal will do as a start – no need for any special traits or strengths. Everyone has something – some way of living more interestingly, of helping others. You only have to take one objective at a time, and realise that there's more pleasure and satisfaction in the doing than in the achieving. It is not the results that are important, but the trying. The actual doing is what brings inner contentment. And if all is well *now*, then that immediately frees you from tomorrow's demands.

These then are our greatest needs, through our goals: self-acceptance, self-appreciation, and then self-celebration, a feeling of joy in our own personal livingness, a bubbling over because I am me – and also a part of you – and just because I am here and alive and experiencing life. And finally we must include self-esteem. We aim to experience none of this of course in

79

a self-satisfied, smug way – but just in a glad feeling of being 'me', of having been chosen to be 'me'. When one can feel that, one is able to offer love freely and unconditionally to others. Because one can rejoice in one's self, one can rejoice in those others also.

A PERMANENT HIGH

Might this be a possible result of reaching our goals, achieving our needs? Perhaps – and why not? Isn't that life's true possibility, perhaps – to be on a permanent high? If we are in tune, unfearful, loving, open to life and expecting the best, who would want more? Not even the greediest persons since, if they felt that way – in tune – they wouldn't be greedy any longer.

Greed: Erich Fromm called this a bottomless pit which exhausts the person in an endless effort to satisfy his needs without ever reaching satisfaction. A greedy person, he said, was always anxiously concerned with himself. He is never satisfied, always restless, driven by the fear of not getting enough, of missing something, of being deprived of something. He is filled with burning envy of anyone who might have more than him. Basically he is a person who is not fond of himself at all but, on the contrary, deeply dislikes himself.

Sai Baba recounts the following peculiar

method of trapping monkeys in India.

'The process consists of bringing a big pot with a small mouth and keeping some material which is attractive to the monkeys inside the pot. A monkey takes a handful of the material and cannot then pull its hand out. It imagines that someone inside the pot is gripping its hand. The monkey has trapped itself because it has taken in its hand such a lot of material. The moment it lets go of the material it could be free. Man binds himself in the same way by grasping and being unable to let go.'

Greed and competitiveness go in concert and competition is related closely to envy and jealousy, insecurity, anxiety and distrust of one's fellow men. But a contented man is, therefore, without greed.

Now we must look at the technique for working on ourselves.

Deep Level and the Ultimate Technique

THE WHOLE-PERSON DEEP LEVEL TECHNIQUE

Before we discuss the A-B-C Ultimate Technique (which is what I call it because I cannot think there can ever be a faster or easier technique), I feel I should show you my previous technique in case you prefer it. It takes longer to learn and master but I consider it the second best technique I know and it may suit some people better.

In Chapter 2, pp 39-41, I showed you how to relax your body and I stress again that you must relax the body before the brain. In the A-B-C Technique you won't need this deliberate relaxation technique since the whole 'system' slips quickly into gear (I use that word deliberately because it really is rather like using an automatic car gear instead of a manual one).

The first thing is to sit comfortably, as upright as you can, with your tail into the back of the chair. Position is not really important. Once you have mastered the technique you can meditate anywhere, at any time – on a bus or train, or even standing up if you need a few seconds' quiet, particularly with the A-B-C method.

What you do need until you become adept is a quiet place where you can be uninterrupted. It is best to meditate regularly, because there is an accumulative effect for good. And if one is working on an actual problem, then the best result will come from meditating at least twice a day for say 15 minutes.

RELAXING THE BRAIN

We have relaxed the body, now for the brain. You have to go to another level of consciousness, to a deeper level of it. In order to help evade that critical censor of your left brain, it is best to go to a deep level which exists somewhere in your mind and is not simply a deep level 'nowhere'. Therefore we shall create the place you go to and call it your 'Serene Scene' –` an imagined or actual nature scene.

I will save the description of your 'Serene Scene' till we discuss the A-B-C Technique, since we need this for both scenarios.

Following on from relaxation of the body the Mindpower Deep Level Technique is obtained through teaching people to count themselves down to that Deep Level. One can use an imaginary escalator or a lift (elevator), but generally I have found my way to be better. One particular pupil preferred to go up rather than down, which only shows how malleable the imagination can be.

I will now run through the instructions as though I am addressing you, but when you have got the hang of it you will be able to instruct yourself mentally in the same way, in your own words. A good way to do it to start with is to record the instructions on a tape recorder. Strangely this plays back to you almost as though it was not your own voice at all. Speak the instructions slowly but firmly, and rather monotonously and it will play back as though someone else is instructing you.

'Your body is now feeling completely relaxed and at peace. Now I want you to visualise (with your eyes closed) that you are in a large room. It is a busy room and there is a hum of noise.

'You wish to be quiet so you move towards the back of the room, towards a smaller room where the interleading door is open. You go in there and close the door behind you, shutting yourself off from the other, larger room.

'Now all is suddenly peaceful and you see a chair

there, a comfortable chair, and you sink into it knowing that you are going to move down, down, inside yourself to a place where you will be completely relaxed, both physically and mentally.

'When I tell you, you will press a button, which is on the arm of the chair, and I will count you down – in your chair – from 10 to 0 and you will then see yourself moving down, deeper and deeper, until at "zero" you will reach a deep level and then you will, in your mind, stand up and step out into your "Serene Scene".

'All right. Press your button now and start moving down, in your chair, as I count you down from 10 to 0. And each time I say a number or the word "deeper" you will go ten times deeper.

Ten . . . Nine . . . Deeper and deeper . . . Eight . . . Deeper still, down, down . . . Seven . . . Deeper and deeper . . . Six . . . Five . . . Feel yourself going deeper, moving down . . . Four . . . Go deeper . . . Three . . . Deeper and deeper . . . Two

. . . One . . . Zero. You are now at a deeper inner level of consciousness and feeling completely relaxed. And now, in your mind, you stand up and move into your Serene Scene. And each time you come here you will be at a still deeper level.'

This then is the Whole-person Deep Level Technique for going into Alpha. Let us now look at the A-B-C Technique and then we can discuss the question of what happens in meditation once the technique has taken us there.

YOUR SERENE SCENE

Before actually going into this technique we ought to explain the concept of the Serene Scene, which is what you will step into with either technique once you have reached the Alpha level.

This is any place chosen by you, usually a nature scene though it could be any private place of relaxation. Perhaps it will be the recall of a place that you have enjoyed visiting and where you have felt at peace. Alternatively, it could be some place you have always fancied being in. It may be some peaceful garden or meadow, somewhere you find particularly soothing, or possibly a quiet beach by the sea. But, wherever it is, when you go there make every detail of your scene so real that you can see the individual blades of grass, the petals on a flower; or see and feel the sand under your feet. Feel the warmth of the sun, the coolness and softness of the grass. Hear the gentle swish and lapping of the sea, a breeze rustling through the trees; envision the blue sky with small white clouds here and there. If there is a pond or stream, take a look at it. Let your mind take you there and really be there!

Lack of Imagination

Some people claim that they have no imagination and cannot picture things, but this is not really true. If you feel you are in this category, close your eyes and go in imagination to a refrigerator and open it and then take from it a lemon. It feels cold in your hand. Look closely at it. Squeeze it and feel how firm it is. Now in your mind go to the kitchen drawer and take out a knife. Cut the lemon in two. Smell it. Bite it and let some of the juice fall on your tongue. Ten to one your mouth is watering. Your body says: 'I'm biting a lemon. It's sour so we must salivate and wash the juice away.'

Well, you see, you told your brain you were eating a lemon. Your brain accepted the instruction and went to work with the body. The brain is not a subtle interpreter; it accepts what it is told. Imagining does not mean trying to project a picture onto your eyelids. But, of course, we 'see' with the brain and not really the eye at all.

A-B-C: The Ultimate Technique

Sit quietly, in a chair that comfortably supports your spine, at least at first while you learn the technique.

Step 1: 'A' stands for 'Above' (or looking upwards, as you will see in a moment).

Step 2: *'B' stands for 'Be Closed'.*
Step 3: *'C' stands for 'Ceal'* (a free version of 'Seal').

Step 1: Breathe deeply two or three times, in and out. Now stare at a point in front of you above your eye level, *but without raising your head.* Say mentally: 'A', knowing this is the first step of three. As you repeat the 'A' you will soon feel your eyes tiring or stinging a little. As you stare, keep saying to yourself: 'A – my eyelids are getting heavy; I will soon want to close my eyes.'

Step 2: As soon as you feel you'd like to close your eyes, do so and say: 'B – Be Closed. They *want* to stay closed. My eyelids are *heavy* and *want* to stay closed.' *Feel* their heaviness.

The secret is that, as also in hypnosis and self-hypnosis, total relaxation of the entire body starts with the closing of the eyes and, importantly, the relaxation of the upper eyelids. Your body just cannot remain tense when your eyelids are relaxed properly. When you 'stare' in Step 1, this is done in order to *tire* the upper eyelid muscles.

Step 3: Now say to yourself: 'C – Ceal' and imagine that your closed eyelids are being *sealed* together with a pleasant, soothing but very sticky and secure (but completely harmless) glue or sealant. *Feel* that your eyelids are so firmly sealed together that you know it would take a real effort to open your eyes.

Don't press your lids tightly together because then you will be taking away their relaxation. Just feel them gummed together but perfectly relaxed.

Your eyelids are now fully relaxed. Let yourself feel this relaxation slowly move down your face, your cheeks, your jaw, then down your neck and shoulders and slowly right down your body to your feet. While doing this relaxation, simultaneously take a deep breath and slowly let it out and feel it flowing right down through your body to your feet. If you run out of breath, take a second one.

After a little practice this whole procedure will probably take about 15 seconds, maybe less.

You now tell yourself: 'I am fully relaxed and at peace.'

Just to recap:

1. 'A – Above': Stare upwards

2. 'B – Be Closed': Close and relax the eyes

3. 'C – Ceal'

From the eyes and eyelids, relaxation now runs down to the feet accompanied by a deep breath.

At first I suggest you now say: 'I am going deeper still.' Then you mentally count yourself *slowly* down from 5 to 0, like this: 'Five . . . Four . . . Deeper and deeper . . . Three . . . Two . . . Deeper still . . . One . . . Zero. I am now at a deep level.' This can be repeated again if you wish. You will now almost certainly be in Alpha.

Your aim in this exercise has been to reach a place called 'Deep Level' where you will be able to step mentally into your Serene Scene. You will recall that this is a remembered or imagined place where you feel happy and peaceful, perhaps a garden or a beach. Come to the same place mentally each time you meditate, so it becomes easy and familiar.

You now visualise yourself stepping into your Serene Scene and then sitting down in a comfortable chair. You have come here either to meditate passively or to work on yourself.

Meditation at Work

FAST TENSION RELIEF

Once you 'get' the A-B-C Technique you can use it in almost any circumstances and wherever you happen to be as an instant 'refresher'. With practice you will only need to close your eyes and sweep the feeling of relaxation from there right down your body, remain in that state for a minute or even less, then tell yourself that when you open your eyes you will feel fully refreshed, alert and full of energy.

For really instant Alpha you can later instruct yourself – while at your Deep Level – that whenever you touch your thumb to your third or ring finger and say to yourself 'Deep Level' you will immediately go there. Do it, practise it, and it will work. Strangely enough you can use this to reserve a parking space, but do it well before you get there (and keep your eyes open!).

USING DYNAMIC MEDITATION

After you have gone into Alpha and your Serene Scene (later on, in Chapter 9, we will move from your Serene Scene into your Power House) you then have the option of either using passive or dynamic meditation, or of using first one and then the other. Since I usually use dynamic meditation first and finish off with passive meditation I am dealing with them in that order.

What is the *feeling* of meditation? It is hard to answer that question since we probably do not all experience it in quite the same way. It seems to me to be experienced at the back of the skull. When we move from Beta to Alpha our consciousness seems to move downwards from the top of one's head until it reaches the Alpha level near the base of the head. The feeling is almost analagous to changing gear in a car. As your brain rhythm shifts down to a slower, calmer level it feels just like a shift in the power of a car.

My personal belief is that when we reach Alpha and want to go to a still deeper state, i.e. Theta, the mind starts to expand outwards, so that it moves from the more confined space of awareness within the skull to embrace also the consciousness that is outside the physical body.

In fact the mind can reach out to the consciousness that is part of everything and everyone.

This depth is not really needed for working dynam
on oneself. The Alpha level is sufficient for that.

USING POSITIVE PHRASES

You are now sitting on a chair (or on the grass
or beach, whatever) in your Serene Scene. You are
enjoying being there, seeing the softness and cool
greenness of the grass, feeling the gentle warmth of the
sun, hearing the slight breeze rustling through the
trees. You can see the blue sky with small clouds here
and there. Just sit for a few moments and feel how
relaxed you are and how much you are at peace there.

You tell yourself and recognise that you are now
at a much deeper and more inward level of mind, near
to the very source of your being. Tell yourself you are
now completely relaxed in body and brain, and that
whenever you instruct yourself to 'relax' *this* is how you
will feel and that you will become more aware and alert
at your inner conscious levels. And you know that you,
yourself, are always in full control.

I want you now to repeat to yourself, in your
mind, one or more positive phrases of this sort for your
own benefit:

*'From now on I shall be continually thinking
positive thoughts that will make me successful, happy, well
and prosperous.'*

'I will be able to use more and more of my mind,

and in such a special way that I shall have full and complete control over my senses and faculties at every level of the mind.'

'From now on my body and my life are free from all disturbing influences. I am at peace.'

'I have all the strength I need to do whatever I have to do, and all ways are open to me.'

'There is peace, harmony and freedom in every situation and in every person with whom I come into contact.'

'I will be using my positive thinking to bring me the understanding and awareness that I desire, so that my improved mental faculties may be used for the good of myself and others, and to serve humanity better.'

COUNTING YOURSELF UP

Before we deal with what you can do and achieve with dynamic meditation, I want to show you the technique for returning to the normal Beta state, or your 'outer levels'.

What you tell yourself in your own words is this, when you have finished your meditation(s): 'I shall now count myself up from 1 to 5 and at 5 I shall open my eyes and feel better, fitter and stronger than before, alert and refreshed and full of energy.' Then you count slowly from 1 to 5, and at 3 you move your fingers and toes, and at 5 you open your eyes.

A MIND SCREEN

Facing you now in your Serene Scene is a large screen, rather like a cinema screen. It is a mental screen on which much of your work on yourself will be done while you are at your Deep Level.

First, what do I mean by working on oneself?

I mean changing bad habits, deprogramming and reprogramming oneself, as we have discussed, to make oneself as one wants to be and can become, improving one's health, and so on.

The reason for using the Mind Screen is as follows. If you sit in your Serene Scene and 'see' yourself there in your mind it is at its most effective if you can really be there in your imagination, seeing and feeling the grass, the flowers, the blue sky, the breeze, the sun. Then if you focus onto an imagined Screen and you see yourself *on* that Screen, since the screen image is twice removed from the actual you sitting in your room that imagined situation somehow becomes a more real situation to your brain. And indeed it is a more focused one than simply visualising and working on yourself. But if you have a preference for one method over another, use it.

You now see your Mind Screen lit up. The first time you try out this technique, project an apple, rather larger than life size, onto the Screen. Blow it up in size so that it becomes quite big. Make it three-dimensional so that you can see all around it. Examine its colour, its stalk and the markings on the skin. Have it turn around so that you can see the back of it and look at it clearly and closely for a few seconds. Take a little time to become really acquainted with your apple. If you prefer, you can use a banana or an orange, or for that matter a flower.

Now while you are sitting there in your Serene Scene, I want you, in your mind, to look down on your lap and see a small electronic control, like a small box with two knobs on it. When you press the first, a picture will appear on the Screen, whatever picture you want.

The second knob, when pressed, will destroy your picture when it needs to be changed. I call this 'Automatic Destruct'.

Remember   Knob No. 1: A New Picture
                 Knob No. 2: Automatic Destruct

Let's see how this works. Suppose you want to change some bad habit of yours. Come to your Deep Level, sit down in your Serene Scene opposite your Mind Screen, light it up and see a picture of yourself as you really are. Tell yourself you are going to change this.

Next, press the second knob, on the right, and the picture will disintegrate.

Press the first knob again and see a new picture

of yourself as you *intend* to be. Tell yourself this is how it will be.

The pictures do not have to be static ones. You can envisage yourself as though in a movie if you wish.

You will be able to use this technique for almost anything. For instance, you can use it if you suffer from nerves when speaking to people or when making a speech. You would first picture yourself being tongue-tied, because of worrying how you will sound or forgetting what you have to say. Always make this first picture a little worse than it really is – exaggerate it. Then destroy it and change the picture to how you want it to be and as it will become. For example, in making a speech, you would see yourself talking easily and in a relaxed way as if you were by yourself or with a close but slightly deaf friend. Then this is how it will happen. Don't forget that you must always first visualise the condition you wish to change.

When you greatly desire something to happen, believe that it will, and expect it to happen. Those are three magic words: **Desire, Believe, Expect - DBE!**

You see, if you desire some attribute, some way of doing things – even something material you need in your life – but believe and expect it will not and cannot happen, then it never will. But when you believe it can, expect that it will and actually see it happening on your Screen, then you start off a chain of changing circumstances that will create whatever you want. This is true and you can accept this truth, knowing that it is indeed so.

This technique can be used to change yourself in any way you wish. We will talk about health later on. But if you want to change anything about yourself – smoking, drinking, the way you work, getting more confidence, playing sport, your attitude to life or to people – you will simply go to your Deep Level and switch on your Mind Screen and see yourself doing what you don't like, or behaving in any way you'd like to change. You tell yourself that you don't like it, that in fact you will simply not have it so. Then you destroy that image and finally see yourself, the *new* you, being as you wish to be, acting as you would wish, as you've always wanted. Do this twice a day and you will soon become the person in the new picture.

DECIDING ONE'S OWN DESTINY

It seems from what we've discussed that one really can do this, certainly as far as is humanly possible. One might believe in fate to a limited extent, in other words that our guidelines are laid out for us but that we can fill in the in-betweens for ourselves. Thus we can plan our goals and make ourselves into the kind of people we want to be. Is that not deciding one's own destiny?

When you find that your past image has in some way not been adequate, correct it. You imagine yourself, on your Screen, as already being the kind of person you wish to be. If for instance you are a fearful and over-anxious person, you will see yourself acting calmly, confidently and with courage. Then you will become what you see. If you recall bad scenarios when you wish you had acted differently to the way you in fact did, re-enact them as you would like them to have occurred. You can't change what another person said or did, but you can correct the way you acted and that would possibly have changed the way the other person behaved.

Suppose you are a writer. If you have any hang-ups about writing, this is the place to get rid of them. The same goes for improving music playing, acting, painting, playing tennis, or golf. For ball games, for example, watch yourself smoothly dealing with the ball, shot by shot. But you must do it in detail – a short movie for this, not just a 'snapshot'. You need to see the perfect contact with the ball, the good feeling of your muscles as you do it, the follow-through, the ball moving exactly to its target, time after time, and people congratulating you after a performance. Did you know that Ben Hogan played every golf stroke in his mind before he made the shot? The renowned Beethoven pianist Artur Schnabel practised even more in his mind than at the piano. Many other successful people have found that working in the mind provides one of the best methods of achievement.

The field is unlimited. Suppose you have a fear of flying. You would go into Alpha – Deep Level, Serene Scene – then visualise yourself on your Mind Screen facing a journey and feeling your usual fear. Next you would destroy that picture and then visualise yourself making a safe, smooth, and enjoyable trip. You'd see yourself actually sitting in comfort, listening to the usual sounds in a plane, looking out and noticing beautiful cloud formations, feeling relaxed and rested. At the same time you would give yourself positive verbal messages. You would repeat this procedure over and over for a couple of weeks, and by then your automatic system would have got the changed message.

CHANGING YOUR LIFE-STYLE

Let us look a little more closely at smoking, drinking, losing weight – if these are things you want to change in your life-style. First you must never forget that you may subconsciously *want* to keep doing the very thing you consciously seem to want to get rid of. Your subconscious may have adopted it as a crutch, just as some people subconsciously adopt an illness, a pain, a paralysed arm. Unless you root this out first, you won't succeed with any kind of therapy, because then you want it more than you don't want it. Of course if you really do want to change, then you can. You can get in touch with your subconscious to find out whether that part of you wants to change, and if not why not. Enquire what 'rewards' you are getting by not changing.

This is how you can do it.

CONTACTING THE SUBCONSCIOUS

Go to your Deep Level. Then just put one hand down on your knee and tell yourself that one of your fingers will represent 'yes' and one 'no'. Now ask yourself which will be your 'yes' finger. After a few seconds one of your fingers will almost certainly move. It may give a preliminary tingle and will then probably give a little jump in the air. Follow the same procedure with your 'no' finger. Finally you can select your 'don't know' finger. Any time you wish to ask your subconscious a question, just ask. This is the way you can learn *why* you do things, what really motivates your actions. If you want to analyse yourself, this is how you can do it.

SMOKING

Let us suppose you honestly decide you want to give up smoking. Go to your Deep Level and see yourself on your Mind Screen. You have already recognised that smoking is bad for you. If necessary you can now convince your subconscious of this and that the rewards of changing are more considerable than anything else. You want to be free of the habit and able to breathe clear, fresh air and be in tune with life. You picture yourself smoking. You know you are wasting money; worse, you are damaging your lungs, making your heart work too fast as your whole system strains to reject and destroy the poison you are putting into your body. You see the smoke swirling and the nicotine and tar inside you filling and choking up your lungs. You are aware of the awful smell of stale tobacco on your skin, on your clothes, in your hair. You see those lungs as black and full of tar from years of smoking. With each puff you can see the tar becoming thicker, spreading to the bronchial tubes and up to the larynx. You hear it rattling as you breathe. *And you refuse to have this!* You say so. You then destroy that picture. You see a new one – of yourself setting a target date on a large calendar. On that ringed day, say a month ahead, you decide you will give up smoking for good. And each time you go to your Deep Level you renew your pledge to that target date. You tell yourself morning and evening that, from that date, you will never smoke again. And when the target date is reached you will just stop, as you have planned. See yourself looking forward to that targeted date and your whole brain and body will combine to make it come true. The imagination must be employed to the full (you can be as innovative and creative as you wish in visualising this scenario).

Perhaps a further picture might be useful here, of yourself *after* the target date being happy and carefree and free from the smoking bond.

ALCOHOL

Deal with alcohol in much the same way as you would with smoking. First ask yourself why you are drinking and realise the benefits of *not* drinking. You would see the bad aspects and after that the good aspects, the picture of oneself as a sober, responsible person actually enjoying life even more without liquor. You would fix a target date on which to stop drinking. Cutting down on drink won't really work; cutting it out is the only satisfactory answer for a person who can finally admit he is dependent on alcohol.

LOSING WEIGHT

Overweight seems a problem for so many people these days because of what we eat and how we eat. Many obese people, of course, have a psychological problem. To put on weight might be a means of 'running away', or of compensating for a lack of love. A little self-analysis would be useful in finding this out. When one finds the cause, that can be dealt with. However, simply to tackle the harmful weight-producing foods is not difficult. You would destroy these on your Mind Screen and tell yourself: *'Never again!'* Realising and accepting that these foods are harmful, you will simply stop eating them. Instruct yourself that every time you see or think of them you will feel an aversion to them because they would be harmful to your body. See the foods with which you will replace them, knowing they will be good for your body and also good to eat. Decide what would be your ideal weight and size and see yourself reaching such a target and looking the way you want to look and *expect* to look. In targeting weight it would be realistic to give yourself a reasonable weekly target, say 2 to 2.5 kilos (or 4 to 5 pounds) reduction a week. When you visualise the picture of yourself you are striving for, tell yourself how good it will feel to be so slim and able to move and walk lightly and easily.

You would say to yourself:

'I will desire and eat only those foods which are good for my body.'

The Health Kick

WHAT CAN YOU CURE?

Did you know that in both England and America there are medical doctors who claim to cure or alleviate cancer, in some cases, through dynamic meditation? In most of these cases they have probably used other remedies too, such as vitamins and dietary changes, but meditation and visualisation are the main tools.

Medical doctors generally seem to have a very narrow vision, due perhaps to their training and the time factor which does not permit them to look deeply into alternative medicine. And they have to be so busy keeping up with drugs that they haven't the space to learn much about the holistic approach and the real healing energies of the body.

There are, of course, exceptions. One of the best known is Dr Carl Simonton of the USA who discovered that he could work best with patients who had an optimistic bent. Everything in life proceeds from a point of view. Dr Selye, the stress expert, related the story of two boys brought up by an alcoholic father. Years later, a psychologist was investigating the effects of drunkenness on children in broken homes. Separately he asked each son how he had developed as he did. The one was a clean-living teetotaller, the other, like his father, a hopeless drunk. And each gave the identical answer:

'What else would you expect when you've had a father like mine?'

So as you can see, it's not *what* happens to you in life that makes the difference, makes you react positively or negatively, but it's the *way* you react. And that is what Dr Simonton found to be the case in cancer patients.

Dr Ian Pearce in England and also the Bristol Clinic use similar therapies.

The patients most likely to succeed with this meditation-plus-visualisation treatment have a strong basic will to live. In meditation (Alpha) they are taught to visualise their tumours and then to visualise their body defences at work and the tumours disappearing. Probably the best way to do this would be to imagine your white cells in action. Whenever there is an injury or invaders have intruded into the body the white cells swarm there in their thousands. See them going there and mopping up, devouring the mass of soft grey renegade cells (that's cancer) cleaning them away. If you like, see the white cells with tiny brooms and pans or, dressed in tiny clean white uniforms, washing the cancer cells away with water hoses, swabbing out the area and chucking them into soakaway gutters for disposal in the body's waste system – or even swallowing them up. The body does not need exact instructions; it just wants the brain to indicate to it what needs to be done and then see the good healthy result, the repaired person in action. You don't have to know or visualise correct anatomy – just use imagination to tell the body what needs to be done. It knows how best to go about it. The patient is required to do this three times a day, and there is a very good success rate.

Another visualisation might be to see the cancer cells in the form of discoloured ice-cubes piled up on a plate in front of the patient. If they are then taken and put in the full glare of the sun, the patient can sit and watch them melt away. Patients learn not to see the cancer cells as being strong with an immune-system image too weak. For instance, one would not use the image of a rock gradually being worn down by a stream of healing water for the process would take too long. A picture of sand-castles collapsed by the tide would obviously be better. One patient used a gardening picturisation, with her white cells plucking out the weeds – the cancer cells.

Always one would end the session with a picture of a complete healing having taken place. This is what the patient is aiming at, the final full healing and not a partial one.

STRENGTHENING THE IMMUNE SYSTEM

A friend of mine had had cancer in the head, for which she was treated with chemotherapy. The treatment was as usual distressingly unpleasant, though it seemed in this case successful. If she had then known about dynamic meditation she could have lessened the bad side-effects by visualising the medicine as defenders aiming weapons against the cancer cells and her body welcoming and accepting the treatment and nullifying its unpleasantness.

Unfortunately she later developed cancer in the spine and was confined to bed. However, she was an artist with a cheerful nature and worked from her bed so that she could still achieve her artistic goals. At this stage I taught her the Whole-person Deep Level Technique. Her brain trouble had left her with an inability to follow numbers so I counted her 'down' merely by using 'deeper' each time a number should have been used, and made a tape for her to use by herself. Very quickly she was up and walking with crutches, and these she was finally able to discard.

She deserved her success and had worked hard. When I had stipulated three times a day she responded by doing it five times. With such enthusiasm, determination and optimism it was difficult to fail. She had been getting rid of her wild cancer cells (they are really renegade cells) by letting her good white cells smother them and take them away.

Cancer cells are weak cells and can only get a hold when the patient's normal defences have become weak through something particularly stressful. Then they begin to multiply. But if one can remain calm and determined, there is every chance that the body will start disposing of them. Dr Ian Pearce, a highly qualified medical man, says we are all likely to get such renegade cells at times, young ones which have forgotten their proper function, perhaps through some chemical imbalance (which can, of course, be stress related or be due to heavy smoking or even aggravated by dietary abuse of the body). All they retain is their ability to multiply. Usually when this happens the body's immune system comes into play, just as it would with any 'foreigners' (for example, a virus), and it isolates and destroys them. But when there's a bad dietary deficiency and/or an emotional breakdown through stress of some kind, then the immune system goes to pieces. *But* the so-called autonomic system, of which the immune system is part, *can* be influenced by deep relaxation and meditation.

Thus you can see that what you think is of great importance to your body's health. And what you think deliberately at your Deep Level will actually get your body moving in the right direction.

Doctors who practise alternative medicine also ask their patients to slowly change to a diet which includes much raw food (vegetables, fruit and probably grain) and to stop eating red meat. In all healing it is important too to rid our minds of any known resentments and hostility. One's mind must be made as peaceful as possible, and meditation and relaxation will, of course, help with that.

MORE HEALING

While cancer is an important matter, there are many other things that badger us – psoriasis, clogged arteries, coughs and colds, headaches, poor eyesight, high or low blood sugar levels, warts and rashes, arthritis, and so on. We cannot guarantee a self-cure for everything but at some time or another everything *has* been cured or alleviated by mind, through brain over body. Whatever the condition, you have first got to learn to really relax the body, and then visualise it performing well and efficiently. Change on your Mind Screen whatever is wrong, in whatever creative way you think best. You *see* a bad, ulcerated throat become pink and well, paint some 'Universal White Healing Balm' on it. Or pick out 'arthritic granules' and gently swab the area with 'Universal Blue Arthritic Solvent'.

Dr Carl Simonton gives the following example in dealing with arthritis:

'First picture your joints very irritated and having little granules on the surfaces. Then see your white blood cells coming in, cleaning up the debris, picking up the little granules and smoothing over the joint surfaces. Then see yourself active, doing what you like to do, free of joint pain.'

HEADACHES

Here is a fine example of the use of dynamic meditation. I used to get a headache almost every day until I used the Alpha plus Screen technique. Now, if I get even the faintest glimmer of one, I simply close my eyes and say:

'I don't get headaches any more. Buzz off!'

It took me about a month or so, concentrating on it hard for at least a fortnight and then easing off, just working at it when I felt the odd headache coming again. This was not a migraine but probably a stress-related headache while doing a fairly intensive job. But the relief, and no more pills! It was worth it.

Besides the normal Mind Screen practice, I also used the time to relax mentally my forehead and neck muscles. Additionally, I used a technique called 'glove anaesthesia' (see p 135-36).

For migraine the best technique is to tell yourself that the blood cells in your head will release their blood and send it down to your hands, which will then become warm and heavy. Feel your hands becoming warmer, just as if they were in quite warm water. The blood *will* come down into your hands and you will almost certainly feel relief in your head.

MORE WHITE CELL IMAGERY

One lady visualises a tiny golden vacuum cleaner inside her body buzzing all around the interior, sucking up all dirt, rubbish and unwanted debris from every possible nook and cranny. She leaves it running even when she is not directing it, thus programming continuous cleansing and healing.

Another patient sees her white cells as a flock of pure white goats. They eat up all 'rubbish' and are strong and tough eaters. Her body she sees as a meadow and the goats are there to keep the place clean. Imagination!

A heart patient saw his troubled blood surging around his heart. The blood was full of sparks of light reaching everywhere. They were in fact his white cells and he visualised them washing over everything, making all clean and perfect. He would watch until the light sparks quietened down and then saw his blood as calm and healthy again. Imagination!

IMAGINATION

This is your key to your health exercises. Imagine! Imagine whatever seems healing and right, and so the process starts for improvement and healing. We must all remember that the brain is a piece of equipment used by the mind. So use it! Tell the brain what it is you want the body to do. DBE: desire to heal yourself, *believe* it can be done, *expect* it to happen – it will!

Don't forget to make your affirmations too. When you see yourself completely well, tell yourself:

'Day by day my disability is getting less and less and I am getting better and better.'

On the Screen, watch yourself make all the movements you desire and completely free from pain. Tell yourself:

'Every day my body will improve in vigour. I feel that life is more purposeful than ever before. I can do and be whatever I want to do or be, provided it does not bring harm to others.'

Tell yourself also that every time you come to your Deep Level and Serene Scene you will come there even more quickly, deeply and easily.

A PROCEDURE, NOT A GIMMICK

This technique is a proper procedure for changing the self, from bad to better, from poor to plenty, from sickness to health. Yes, in this life you can do what you want to do, achieve what you set out to achieve (but do remember that the journey is far more important than the arrival). We in fact already do this unconsciously, so why not consciously? If we set out to have riches, or a new car, and we concentrate on achieving that, see ourselves doing it, in Alpha, then it must happen in due course. The necessary circumstances will eventuate.

Personally, I consider it is a wasteful use of a wonderful tool to penny-pinch and say: 'I want £1,000 or whatever.' It's much, much better to create the circumstances whereby one can do a good job, produce something worth while – something for people to see, read, use, hear or eat – and then the rewards must come. Money is merely the natural token of abundance for doing something well, providing good service, for putting what Solzhenitsyn calls 'duty' before what so many people seem to think of as their 'rights'.

SLEEP

If you feel yourself becoming sleepy while in Alpha (and you shouldn't), shake your head from side to side for a moment and it will clear. But if you want to use Alpha for going to sleep at night, go 'down' and then count yourself deeper and deeper. Tell yourself, *'Let go, let go'*, and then instruct yourself that you are now in self-hypnosis and will simply drift into normal sleep – and you will.

ME AND THE IMMUNE SYSTEM

It is interesting to note that Dr William Weir, Consultant Physician of the Royal Free Hospital, London, says:

'One of the cornerstones of any therapeutic regimes for ME (myalgic encephalomyelitis, also known as the chronic fatigue syndrome) involves a regime of rest and relaxation. It is comparatively easy to rest in the strict physical sense but it is the psychological dimension which eludes many people. A meditation technique is therefore invaluable in this situation as it helps provide the missing dimension. Interestingly, some individuals with ME may first experience a transient worsening of their symptoms before noticing an improvement. One explanation for this is that the meditation in some way "switches on" a hitherto unresponsive component of the immune system, enabling it to fight the chronic virus infection present . . .With time, these symptoms abate as the immune system clears the offending virus.'

Your Power House

WHAT IT IS AND WHY

We are now going to move you from your Serene Scene to your Power House. It is best to work through and use your Serene Scene for a while since the Power House concept is a little more advanced. Because of this your brain will accept the latter more readily after it has become used to the idea of creating something entirely out of your imagination. It easily accepts the Serene Scene concept because this is probably some scene it has encountered before and is familiar with.

You are now going to create something that you will be able to use for the rest of your life, although you can always change it if you wish. This is going to be a more concentrated place than your Serene Scene and it will be easier to work there on various projects.

Other people have created such places. Einstein was said to have a mental laboratory, where he went to work on different problems. Napoleon Hill had a 'cabinet room' and used to consult, mentally, several famous people there. I myself used to have a private room in my mind for passive meditation. Then I created another for dynamic meditation. At first I actually used to lock the door; that's how real it was for me. Eventually I realised this was rather ridiculous and dismantled the lock. I had one room with clear, unbreakable glass on top of a mountain and the other one somewhere else. When it seemed silly to me to have two such places I decided to combine them.

It really doesn't matter where you construct your Power House or what it is built of – brick, stone, wood, glass – and it will be furnished in any way you like. I had one pupil who built her Power House under the sea. She first had to go onto a small island and then go down below to reach it.

The way to go about it is this. Go to your Deep Level and then go even deeper inside yourself; then tell yourself that from this deep level of consciousness you have the power to do anything your imagination can conceive, always for good, for yourself and for others.

CREATING IT

Now see yourself walking down three steps (you won't need the use of a stick if you are walking in your mind!) and then you see (in fact you create) a door in front of you; this is the entrance to your Power House. Thus, whenever you wish afterwards, you can go down to your Deep Level and walk, mentally, down those three steps and come to your Power House, which is wherever you want it to be and in whatever surroundings you choose.

Now you open the door and go inside. And now you are really there and building, creating, the four main walls and the ceiling and floor of your personal Power House. It is best to take a little time on creating this, making it whatever size and shape you want but leaving one wall clear because this is where your Mind Screen will be. Use whatever materials you desire. Put a carpet on the floor if you want, and have a window or windows as you like, and curtains or pictures. The lighting will come on automatically as you enter the room, though you can always control it (for example, to make it dimmer if you want to do passive meditation). And the temperature will always be comfortable. Remember that you are both architect and builder so the details are yours to command. And, of course, if you want to add, change or remodel you can do so at any time you are in your Power House level.

When you are in Alpha Deep Level, time has a different quality and probably five minutes will be ample to erect your Power House. When it is done you will be ready for the furnishing of it. The one thing you will definitely need is, of course, your Mind Screen. This will be quite large and will light up well whenever you use it, and you will be able to see anything or anyone (including yourself) on it in three dimensions, in full length or close up, and still or moving, as you wish. You can screen a personal movie on it to review some incident in the past or to project into the future to plan total success, as well as seeing the present, of course.

You will need at least one comfortable chair and perhaps a nice desk or table. You will usually sit in your chair. Make it just the kind you want so you can sit comfortably in it while watching your Screen. It is a good idea to have a panel built into the arm of the chair for your Screen controls – one to produce new pictures and the second one to destroy them.

If you are imaginative enough you can, of course, have a radio on your desk and listen there to your favourite music. And there are many devices you may wish to have accessible, perhaps a delicate brush to sweep away any germs, infection, or even facial lines you don't want. Have a whole array behind you of special lotions for applying to any injury for cleansing and fast healing, and label them, e.g. 'Universal Throat Paint', or 'Universal Arthritis Paint', or 'Universal Anaesthetic Ointment'). In fact, you can use anything you can imagine or invent.

To the right of your Screen, in the far wall, I suggest you construct a door. You may at some time invite someone in to assist you (a doctor, a counsellor?), or you may go through there yourself, as I'll explain later.

YOUR FIRST EXERCISE

If you go and sit down in your Power House and observe your Screen lighted up, you can visualise yourself on it. See it as though it is a moving X-ray of yourself. As you watch, see your skull, the eyes in your skull, and your jawbone, and then see inside your neck and the bones in your shoulders. You glance down and you can see your digestive tract going down to your stomach, and then you see your respiratory tract going down to your lungs which are breathing rhythmically. You see your ribs and, behind them, you glimpse your heart beating in a normal and natural way. And then you move your eyes slowly down your body, becoming aware of each organ, and your arms and fingers, your thighs, legs, ankles and toes. Now you turn around on your Screen and you, the watcher. Your eyes move slowly up again, seeing your legs, thighs, the pelvis and the spine, up to the neck and back to the skull again.

And you feel now that you can always examine yourself in this way if you wish, if you believe anything to be wrong, and you can discover what is wrong and start healing it. Just for a moment see and feel healing energy entering your head and running right through your body. You might envisage it as a white or a golden light pouring into you.

And now it is time to count you up to your conscious level. You will know that if you use your Power House and your tools properly you can easily programme yourself for success and health in any way you desire.

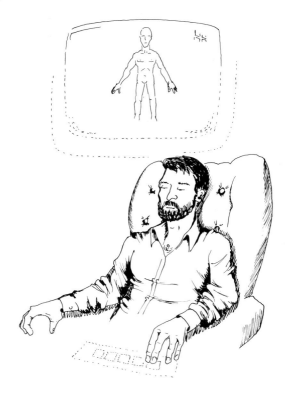

Passive Meditation

'How can man extend his range of consciousness? I believe that human beings experience a range of mental states which is as narrow as the middle three notes of a piano keyboard. I believe that the possible range of mental states is as wide as the whole piano keyboard, and that man's sole aim and business is to extend his range from the usual three or four notes to the whole keyboard.'

Colin Wilson, RELIGION AND THE REBEL

THE HUB OF LIFE

Herbert Puryear in REFLECTIONS ON THE PATH (which deals with Edgar Cayce's readings) said that meditation (meaning passive meditation) is not only the hub of healing but should be the hub of our lives. Yet, he added, it may be the most talked about and least practised of the activities recommended by every spiritual teacher.

Krishnamurti when asked by Fritjof Capra: *'How can I be a scientist and still follow your advice of stopping thought and attaining freedom from the known?'* replied: *'First you are a human being; then you are a scientist. First you have to become free and this freedom cannot be achieved through thought. It is achieved through meditation – the understanding of the totality of life in which every form of fragmentation has ceased.'*

A scientist specialises in some part of life, but needs to see and understand it as a whole first so that he can realise just where his speciality will fit in. When you meditate you are in the centre of consciousness.

'Meditation,' wrote Aldous Huxley, *'has been used in every part of the world, and from the remotest periods, as a method for acquiring knowledge about the essential nature of things.'*

A young graduate student on his way to a meditation course said:

'It's the greatest adventure of all. You don't know what you're going to find, but whatever it is you know it's going to change your life.'

'Meditation is not an escape from daily living', said writer Ardis Whitman, *'but a preparation for it, and what is of surpassing importance is what we bring back from the experience.'*

The psychologist Erich Fromm, asked for a practical solution to the problems of living, replied:

'*Quietness. The experience of stillness. You have to stop in order to be able to change direction.*'

Ardis Whitman wrote: '*Meditation is not a cure-all. Properly used however it can give us back the wonderland of our minds . . . Today there is a widespread feeling that the world of tomorrow should be very different from the world of today. Meditation is seen as a prelude to that transformation – a way of preparing for it, a way of changing lives and thus changing the world.*'

IS MEDITATION RELIGION?

No, it is not. But if you are interested in the concept, perhaps you should ask yourself why. Is it to learn to allay tension (which of course it can)? Is it only to improve your health? If it is, you need only concern yourself with dynamic (or practical) meditation. If you are not afraid to face or accept the possibility, even probability, of a directing Force outside yourself, a Universal Consciousness of which you are a part, then you can do no harm but only good by opening yourself to that Consciousness.

USING PASSIVE MEDITATION

Herbert Puryear gives an illustration of how he uses meditation.

'*As I meditate in the morning, my mind drifts off to an afternoon job interview about which I am concerned.*

First I acknowledge the fact of my mind drifting.'

(He does not stop the drift because he is unwittingly seeking a solution to a problem and seizes the opportunity so offered. But it is possible to stop the 'drift' of stray thoughts if you wish, as I shall show you.)

'Second,' he goes on, *'I invite the spirit of Christ – or God – to stand between me and the situation. I say: "Lord, this is important. I know it can be handled only in Your Presence. I cannot handle it but I know You can." And third, I say: "Because this is important, it is all the more reason why I need to take these few moments to become centred . . ." In an ongoing practice of meditation, we begin to put our concerns into relationship with the Divine and release the concern to Him. For example, let's say that every Thursday afternoon you have an appointment with Joe, with whom you are having difficulties. In your meditation during the week, if your mind drifts off to your concern with Joe, you try to sense the presence of the [Universal Power] in this relationship. In your next meeting with him, instead of making the usual negative responses, you will find yourself responding to him with a more loving attitude. Why? Because you have relinquished your anxiety. You know that there is another Power working in the relationship. You are more loving and Joe responds by being more cooperative.'*

In this sort of context the Santa Fe Stress Clinic recommends that after meditation you use a technique which they call 'Fill your Heart with Loving Thoughts'.

'A loving heart,' they say, 'will help to heal many of our ills. Begin with thoughts of family and friends. They are easier to love, usually, than strangers or enemies. As a face appears before you, or a name, send your blessings and loving thoughts to that person. Then devote some time to sending loving thoughts to those who may be causing you some disturbance. Try to understand clearly that they are fumbling through life as we all are and our anger and bitterness towards them only hurts us all. Forgive and forget so that you can be free of anger. The two or three minutes you put into sending out loving thoughts is very important and you will reap tremendous benefit to your state of health as well as your peace of mind.'

SPIRITUAL PROGRESS

If you are concerned with spiritual progress you will be interested in what Joel Goldsmith, an inspired healer and teacher, had to say:

'Without meditation it is difficult if not almost impossible to make spiritual progress, because spiritual attainment is accomplished in the mind. It was revealed to me that the best way to attain divine consciousness lies in meditation . . . To attain through meditation, there must first of all be an agreement within one's self that in the meditation there is no seeking for any thing or condition, but a seeking only for the illumined mind . . .'

Although this seems a different viewpoint to others we have mentioned, it must be remembered that Joel Goldsmith was concerned very strictly with pure spiritual progress for the individual and nothing else. Ideally, if you have learnt simply to 'hand over' in deepest faith, he is probably correct.

On the question of illumination, Dr Raynor Johnson, in A RELIGIOUS OUTLOOK FOR MODERN MAN, says:

'Mystical experience, in which for a moment the centre of the soul contacts a Reality higher than oneself – the Spirit – is a state of Illumination which we are all seeking, whether we know it or not. Everything that we can desire in our highest moments is satisfied in this union . . . The goal of mind control is important; the particular method used to reach the goal is not . . . Those who have trodden this path and finally come to glimpse the Reality which lies beyond mind tell us that it is unforgettable, peaceful, satisfying, and blissful beyond the power of words to describe . . . But whatever inner discipline is undertaken, the outer life has concurrently to be lived in the right way . . . If a person's daily round is dull and uninspiring let him say: "I do it gladly because it is my duty; I do it because it is my offering of service to God."

If a person's daily round is interesting let him in gratitude offer his work as a service to God, not concerned with benefit to himself but with help to others.'

127

PURPOSE OF MEDITATION

Edgar Cayce, asked by a patient if he could receive guidance from meditation, replied:

'On any subject! Whether you are going digging for worms or playing a concerto.'

Dr Puryear comments:

'The answer to every question, every problem, is within; there is no question too great or too small to bring to the One within.' He adds: *'Some worry about the dangers of meditation, but let us say that the only thing more dangerous than meditating is not meditating.'*

Ramala, in THE REVELATIONS OF RAMALA, says much the same:

'As you are faced with the problems of the day you should consciously tune into the Higher Self . . . Meditation is the key to your evolution. It is the only key for, until you have unlocked the door to your Higher Consciousness, truly you will not discover the meaning of life on this earth.'

Finally, before discussing the technique of passive meditation, listen to Dr Puryear's interesting summing up of the reason why the power to meditate was given to us:

'In the study of biology one finds that the human body is fantastically adapted to life on the earth. It is a special instrument for coping with and expressing mastery and creativity in the earth plane. It is also another special kind of instrument. We may think of it as God's special

solution to a problem: His children as spiritual beings cutting themselves off from the awareness of His nature. Because we had been placed in a three-dimensional plane, it became necessary to develop an instrument that could manifest in such a plane, and yet one which had the capability for the awareness of oneness with the Infinite. There had to be the sensory potentiality for experiencing that awareness in consciousness.'

This capability of awareness with the Whole, a way of becoming aware of our oneness with our Creator, of silent communication, of receiving 'input', is the true purpose of passive meditation.

THE MEDITATION, PLUS THOUGHT CONTROL

At your Deep Level you now step down your three steps to your Power House. You open the door and sit in your particular chair facing your Mind Screen. However, this time you are not there in your Power House to 'work' but to contact the stillness which is at your own centre. As you sit in your chair you dim the lights a little and you close your eyes and feel at peace, and you know you are going to sit there in the quiet of your own inner room, your refuge, and you are going to just be aware. And if anything comes to you it will simply just happen and you will experience it and enjoy it; otherwise you will simply sit in peace and stillness and with absolute calm in your mind.

You are now getting in touch with your inner self. Whenever you do this, if a thought should arise from your brain, you will watch the thought float up by your head and you will immediately put a 'balloon' around it – just mentally draw a line around the thought and so encase it in a balloon – and as soon as you do this it will drift right away from you, float away and vanish. You will do this whenever a thought occurs from your brain, enclose it in a balloon and then watch it quickly float away and vanish. If it is a troublesome thought or vision of someone, you can just 'pop' the balloon with your finger.

An alternative is to imagine your mind as a piece of glass on which your thought picture arrives. You can then wipe it away with a mental windscreen wiper. Another technique is to breathe fast four times, in and out, and the thought will disappear. A final method is to put invisible armour around your head, or a white light, through which no thought can penetrate. Use whichever method appeals most to you.

Soon you will find that thoughts become discouraged and will stop coming. In this way you can control the production of thought, and then you will be able to sit in contact with your inner self and experience that feeling of peace and perhaps joy which comes to you, or any other good experience.

And often when you come to your Power

House like this you will feel and know that there is a Presence there with you, a Higher Self, a seen or unseen Presence or Teacher whom you can consult when you feel the need, a Presence who is there only when you ask and who has only your good in mind.

And you know that you can have this experience of meditation whenever you wish and then you can sit there as long as you wish, or you can set a time limit if you so instruct yourself. Or you can just decide when it is time to move from there because your mind, though still and at peace, will be alert and aware, and you can easily go back to your outer level whenever you wish by slowly counting up from 1 to 5, knowing you will feel very well indeed when you open your eyes, and then opening them at the count of 5.

BEYOND MEDITATION

After you have experienced the above I would like you to try one final step, something a little more advanced. You go to your Deep Level as before and then into your Power House. And now I will show you how to go beyond meditation, to go outwards instead of inwards.

So now, in your Power House you stand up and go forward and then you walk to the door on the right of your Screen and open it. And when you open it you create a balcony onto which you can go. Then you walk onto the balcony, and you see that you are high up, high above the Earth, which you can see below you when you look down (perhaps you are in the clouds, or above the clouds, or high above mountains). And then you sit down on a chair on your balcony and tell yourself you are going to a deeper level than ever before, you are going deeper and deeper within yourself. You can feel that you are at a much deeper level of consciousness than you were before, and it is a very good, strong feeling.

And now for a while you are going to leave your body sitting there as your mind goes out to join the power of the Life Force which is there. You say to yourself, 'There is only God; there is only God's power,' which is an absolute protection for you. And then you feel that your mind moves and goes out from your body to that great Power – and now you are one with It, and listening and aware, and open to experience anything which comes to you and which can only be good.

You realise that your mind is now high above the earth, that everything which happens there is not your immediate concern, not while you are here, that you are part of the Universal Mind, a part of the Infinite which is immortal. You are aware now that all things on the earthly sphere pass with time. You know that while you are part of that, too, you are also part of the eternal whole, and you feel cherished and unique, and yet a part of the great unity of all things and beings on this earth and within the universe.

And as you remain there you know that you can come here and experience this whenever you wish and for as long as you wish, and, as before, you can go back to your outer level whenever you are ready by counting yourself up from 1 to 5, when you will feel very well, refreshed, alert and full of energy.

TAPING

If possible, tape the meditation techniques and use that for a while, or else just use your own words and thoughts.

Additional Techniques

SELF-HYPNOSIS

In Chapter 4, page 62 I referred briefly to going into a still lower brain rhythm for deeper self-instruction. Normally you would not need this depth, but it can be useful in certain circumstances. If you have an emergency – a sudden pain or injury that you want to deal with quickly and in deep concentration – you could well use the technique I will describe. Sometimes I use it to induce sleep in the middle of the night if I wake up and thoughts start whirling around.

You tell yourself that you are going to induce self-hypnosis, and that it will, in the case of sleep, automatically take you into a normal deep sleep until your usual waking time in the morning. The following is the best and simplest methods I have discovered.

First, tell yourself you are going to count up to 10 and that you will then be in a state of hypnotic sleep. Now open your eyes and strain them a little by looking upwards without moving your head. As soon as your eyes tire a little, close them and say 'One' to yourself. Open them again, repeat the process but say 'Two'. Then 'Three', 'Four', and so on. You will find that the time of leaving your eyes open becomes progressively shorter, until you would rather not open them again - probably at about the count of 'Five'. Carry on counting without opening your eyes again and at 'Ten' tell yourself you are now in a state of self-hypnosis.

If you are using self-hypnosis for any reason other than sleep, you can now instruct your body as you wish. For example, 'The pain in my leg is going away now and my natural body defences will work quickly to repair any damage.' Stay 'there' for a little while and then, when you feel more comfortable, tell yourself that your leg will continue to improve as you now open your eyes. Then of course you could add whatever treatment you would normally give.

GLOVE ANAESTHESIA

An alternative way of dealing with pain is to induce what is called 'glove anaesthesia'. You can anaesthetise one hand but it is simplest to do it with one finger – probably your first or index finger. Tell yourself in self-hypnosis that it is going to become de-sensitised and numb, without feeling. As you repeat this, try to sense the finger losing all feeling. Probably it will start by tingling, and then gradually losing feeling. Test it by pressing your thumbnail into it. When it feels fairly numb, instruct yourself that when you touch whatever part of your body is painful the anaesthesia will transfer itself to that part. Talk to yourself as you rub your finger over the affected area, stressing that you are anaesthetising wherever you rub and also below the skin, and that this will last until healing begins. Glove anaesthesia works very well for headaches. Tell yourself you are transferring the sensation of anaesthesia from the first finger to the site of your headache and touch your head accordingly.

Problem Solving

This is a non-meditative technique which I recalled only because of treating someone. It is a 'handing-over' technique which I published as a tiny booklet but I realise now that it would be even more effective if done in Alpha. I went to see June, a woman of about 50 who had an appalling history of back trouble. She had had two operations and many scans, X-rays, dyes, and all the rest of it. She now had almost constant pain, which you could see in her eyes and from the wastage of her body. The doctors had given her up as a case of 'psychosomatic illness' (could that be something for the medicos to *give up?*), and in fact one young idiot of a hospital resident actually said to her:

'Can you tell me how it feels to be a psychosomatic case?'

Well, I told her there was little I could do. I tried to induct her into meditation, even hypnosis (which I am better at now than I was then). But though she tried, she said, she just couldn't concentrate. And whenever I went to see her (she was limited to movement around her flat), she spent what little time we had together railing against fate, the many doctors she had seen, and her husband, whose tolerance and help had worn thin – he was just not strong enough to be the rock she had need of.

In short she was – or had become – a very negative person. But I fully sympathised with her and understood the circumstances which had made her so. I was afraid she might take her life. She didn't, but it was always a possibility and slowly I became less sympathetic and less understanding – rather like her husband, I suppose. If she wasn't so darned negative, I thought, she might be able to start on a positive recovery programme. She might never be fully cured but it could become more tolerable. That was my thinking.

We now come to me.

I have a weakness in my lower back and one day I lifted a really heavy garden pot full of earth. I

137

moved it blithely from left to right and my body was wrongly placed for the movement. I was an idiot. I felt something give. Two days later I was in agony and could hardly move for fear of going into spasm.

In bed I tried to meditate and succeeded to some degree – after all, I have had a lot of experience. But the back got worse. Things sometimes do at first, stirred by new energies, but I hadn't come near to being able to give myself a proper treatment. Two days later, still in bed, I became morose, depressed. I did not know what I had really done to my back. I had thought I'd pulled a muscle, perhaps torn some tissue. Now I began to think I had done something much worse, perhaps slipped a disc, crushed a nerve. My whole middle was on fire. It was pain to get up, pain to lie down, and when I moved about at all I merely crept. Perhaps I would never recover properly. I lay still and could scarcely think.

Suddenly I remembered June.

My God, if this was what she felt like! And I had expected her, without previous introduction or training, to be positive! And now here was I, giving up. At least she hadn't done that.

Then I remembered my little four-step problem-solving technique. A way to 'hand over'. I needed it.

Here it is:

Step 1. You have a seemingly insoluble problem. Clearly 'see' or visualise the problem (or condition which needs healing or changing) in your mind.

Step 2. Imagine a key with, at the top, a circle containing a cross or any other symbol of Infinite Power. Tell yourself:

'There is a key to every problem.'

Step 3. Move your eyes and mind up to that symbol and say:

'I now release this problem (condition) to Infinite Power in the certainty that it will be resolved. I know I can hand over this problem in this way and, because I so ask, it is already being resolved.'

Step 4. To demonstrate your faith, you give thanks for the solution or healing which is to come.

At once I carried out the four-step process and immediately I felt better. The pain was still there but my mind cleared. I felt positive and I knew that it was only a matter of patience and my back would get better. Then I could perform my Mind Mirror healing with ease and with absolute knowledge of positive results to come, as they did.

HELPING OTHERS

You can use the four-step technique for aiding others. In meditation you can also often help or even heal others. You can send healing energy, however you visualise this. I myself like gold, which you can also surround your house or car or others with for protection, though some prefer to use a white light. You can also send 'thought forms', as long as they are for the benefit of others and not merely yourself. For instance, in a very difficult child or a troublesome adult you can visualise that person and send suggestions for better behaviour. The more explicit you are the more likely they are to be effective.

* * *

A LAST WORD:

Don't Delay - Meditate Today!

The Quantum Project:

Quality and integrity, dedicated to the realisation of
human potential and its practical application.

If you've enjoyed reading this book from Quantum,
you will enjoy the other titles listed. Covering many
subject areas, particularly that of Self Development and
Personal Psychology, there are plenty to choose from.
Look out for other popular titles available from
Quantum.

APPLIED VISUALISATION
AUTHOR: **James Lynn Page**
ISBN: 0-572-01555-0 Price: **£6.95**

Applied Visualisation is a must for anyone with an interest in the inner mind and the creative process. The techniques are of immense value in developing creative potential.

This practical work programme and text is the product of new research into the nature of the mind, and demonstrates the successful practice of Applied Visualisation.

Visualisation techniques have become widely accepted within many schools of modern psychology, where they are used effectively both for personal growth and self-exploration.

Used also in meditation and healing, the effects of Visualisation are acknowledged but little understood. Until now that is. Here is the definitive revelation of how and why Visualisation can fulfil the wishes of the individual. The direct and dramatic effect that Applied Visualisation has on personal life circumstance is accurately described. From this it is but a short step to fulfilling your own potential.

Other titles by W. Foulsham & Co. Ltd.
SUCCESSFUL PROBLEM SOLVING
AUTHOR: **Dean Juniper**
ISBN: 0-572-01319-1 Price: **£5.99**

In each of us there lies a source of creative energy. In most of us, however, it has become too deeply buried to be unlocked without expert guidance.

Dean Juniper, an Educational Psychologist, shows us how to rediscover this hidden source and to realise our full creative potential. With it we can solve emotional *and* business problems more effectively, make creative decisions with greater confidence and find original ways in which to organise our life and our work *successfully*.

Illustrated throughout with case histories that show how the various methods and techniques can be applied to everyday situations. It then carefully defines the type of problem and then suggests the road to its solution. Charts and questions help us to define our own problem areas and to tackle them *creatively*, be they personal, emotional or professional.

The author has carefully considered effective and helpful ways of overcoming problems in relating to other people, or arising from personal characteristics. He enables us to deal with feelings of guilt, anxieties concerning mental or physical fitness, memory lapses and various additions.

A highly valuable book for anyone wishing to lead a full and more rewarding life.

DIRECT YOUR SUBCONSCIOUS
AUTHOR: **Paul Harris**
ISBN: 0-572-01573-9 Price: **£4.99**

Success isn't something that happens naturally - we all have to work for it. Yet sometimes this is easier said than done. In this book, Paul Harris shows us that through SRT - Subconscious Reprogramming Technique, you can help yourself towards your own personal success.

Through a series of fascinating, yet simple exercises you will be able to turn personal limitations and insecurities into successful achievements, and direct your subconscious to work for you all the way.

Whatever your goals, now you can achieve them.

Give up smoking..... Reduce stress.....
Recover from depression.....

Achieve these and many more with this personal workbook to map your course to success.